D1539032

Adoption

OPPOSING VIEWPOINTS®

Other Books of Related Interest

OPPOSING VIEWPOINTS SERIES

Abortion
American Values
Animal Rights
Child Abuse
Child Welfare
Culture Wars
Domestic Violence
The Family
Homosexuality
Interracial America
Male/Female Roles
Population
Sex
Teenage Pregnancy
Teenage Sexuality
Teens at Risk
Welfare

CURRENT CONTROVERSIES SERIES

The Abortion Controversy
Child Abuse
Family Violence
Gay Rights
Reproductive Technologies
Teen Pregnancy and Parenting

AT ISSUE SERIES

The Ethics of Abortion
Gay Marriage
Interracial Relationships
Sex Education
Single-Parent Families
Teen Sex
Welfare Reform

Adoption

OPPOSING VIEWPOINTS®

Roman Espejo, *Book Editor*

Daniel Leone, *President*
Bonnie Szumski, *Publisher*
Scott Barbour, *Managing Editor*

OPPOSING
VIEWPOINTS®
SERIES

Greenhaven Press, Inc., San Diego, California

Cover photo: Eyewire

Library of Congress Cataloging-in-Publication Data

Adoption / Roman Espejo, book editor.
    p. cm. — (Opposing viewpoints)
    Includes bibliographical references and index.
    ISBN 0-7377-0789-5 (pbk. : alk. paper) —
ISBN 0-7377-0790-9 (lib. : alk. paper)
    1. Adoption—United States—Psychological aspects.
2. Adoption—Moral and ethical aspects—United States.
3. Adoption—Government policy—United States. I. Espejo,
Roman, 1977– II. Series.

HV875.55 .A3647 2002
362.73'4'0973—dc21   2001040358
                                                              CIP

Greenhaven Press, Inc., P.O. Box 289009
San Diego, CA 92198-9009

"Congress shall make no law...abridging the freedom of speech, or of the press."

First Amendment to the U.S. Constitution

The basic foundation of our democracy is the First Amendment guarantee of freedom of expression. The Opposing Viewpoints Series is dedicated to the concept of this basic freedom and the idea that it is more important to practice it than to enshrine it.

Contents

Why Consider Opposing Viewpoints?   8

Introduction   11

Chapter 1: Should Adoption Be Encouraged?

Chapter Preface   16

1. Adoption Should Be Encouraged   17
   Elizabeth Bartholet

2. Adoption Should Be Abolished   25
   Evelyn Burns Robinson

3. Adoption Is an Alternative to Abortion and
   Single Parenting   32
   Marvin Olasky

4. Adoption Is Not an Alternative to Abortion   38
   Katha Pollitt

Periodical Bibliography   42

**Chapter 2: Whose Rights Should Be Protected in
   the Adoption Process?**

Chapter Preface   44

1. The Rights of Birth Mothers Must Be Protected   45
   Heather Lowe

2. The Rights of Birth Fathers Must Be Protected   55
   Jeanne Warren Lindsay

3. The Rights of Adoptive Parents Must Be Protected   63
   Madelyn Freundlich and Lisa Peterson

4. The Rights of the Child Must Be Protected   72
   L. Anne Babb

Periodical Bibliography   79

**Chapter 3: What Types of Adoption Should Be
   Encouraged?**

Chapter Preface   81

1. Transracial Adoptions Should Be Encouraged   83
   Kirsten Wonder Albrecht

2. Same-Race Adoptions Should Be Encouraged   91
   Leslie Doty Hollingsworth

3. Gay and Lesbian Couples Should Have the Right
   to Adopt   102
   Jill M. Crawford

4. Gay and Lesbian Parenting May Not Be
   Beneficial   113
   Lynn D. Wardle

Periodical Bibliography   126

Chapter 4: Should Adoption Policies Be Changed?

Chapter Preface   128

1. Adoption with Clear Familial Boundaries Is Best   129
   Mary Beth Seader and William L. Pierce

2. An Open Adoption Policy Is Best   137
   James L. Gritter

3. Adoption Records Should Remain Sealed   146
   Ira Carnahan

4. Adoption Records Should Be Opened   154
   Denise K. Castellucci

5. Policies Should Emphasize Family Preservation   161
   National Coalition for Child Protection Reform

6. Policies Should Not Emphasize Family
   Preservation   172
   Amanda Spake

7. The Internet Should Be Used to Recruit Adoptive
   Families   181
   Children's Bureau

8. Internet Adoption Remains a Gray Area   189
   Frances Grandy Taylor

Periodical Bibliography   194

For Further Discussion   195
Organizations to Contact   197
Bibliography of Books   200
Index   202

Why Consider Opposing Viewpoints?

"The only way in which a human being can make some approach to knowing the whole of a subject is by hearing what can be said about it by persons of every variety of opinion and studying all modes in which it can be looked at by every character of mind. No wise man ever acquired his wisdom in any mode but this."

John Stuart Mill

In our media-intensive culture it is not difficult to find differing opinions. Thousands of newspapers and magazines and dozens of radio and television talk shows resound with differing points of view. The difficulty lies in deciding which opinion to agree with and which "experts" seem the most credible. The more inundated we become with differing opinions and claims, the more essential it is to hone critical reading and thinking skills to evaluate these ideas. Opposing Viewpoints books address this problem directly by presenting stimulating debates that can be used to enhance and teach these skills. The varied opinions contained in each book examine many different aspects of a single issue. While examining these conveniently edited opposing views, readers can develop critical thinking skills such as the ability to compare and contrast authors' credibility, facts, argumentation styles, use of persuasive techniques, and other stylistic tools. In short, the Opposing Viewpoints Series is an ideal way to attain the higher-level thinking and reading skills so essential in a culture of diverse and contradictory opinions.

In addition to providing a tool for critical thinking, Opposing Viewpoints books challenge readers to question their own strongly held opinions and assumptions. Most people form their opinions on the basis of upbringing, peer pressure, and personal, cultural, or professional bias. By reading carefully balanced opposing views, readers must directly confront new ideas as well as the opinions of those with whom they disagree. This is not to simplistically argue that everyone who reads opposing views will—or should—change his or her opinion. Instead, the series enhances readers' understanding of their own views by encouraging confrontation with opposing ideas. Careful examination of others' views can lead to the readers' understanding of the logical inconsistencies in their own opinions, perspective on why they hold an opinion, and the consideration of the possibility that their opinion requires further evaluation.

Evaluating Other Opinions

To ensure that this type of examination occurs, Opposing Viewpoints books present all types of opinions. Prominent spokespeople on different sides of each issue as well as well-known professionals from many disciplines challenge the reader. An additional goal of the series is to provide a forum for other, less known, or even unpopular viewpoints. The opinion of an ordinary person who has had to make the decision to cut off life support from a terminally ill relative, for example, may be just as valuable and provide just as much insight as a medical ethicist's professional opinion. The editors have two additional purposes in including these less known views. One, the editors encourage readers to respect others' opinions—even when not enhanced by professional credibility. It is only by reading or listening to and objectively evaluating others' ideas that one can determine whether they are worthy of consideration. Two, the inclusion of such viewpoints encourages the important critical thinking skill of objectively evaluating an author's credentials and bias. This evaluation will illuminate an author's reasons for taking a particular stance on an issue and will aid in readers' evaluation of the author's ideas.

It is our hope that these books will give readers a deeper understanding of the issues debated and an appreciation of the complexity of even seemingly simple issues when good and honest people disagree. This awareness is particularly important in a democratic society such as ours in which people enter into public debate to determine the common good. Those with whom one disagrees should not be regarded as enemies but rather as people whose views deserve careful examination and may shed light on one's own.

Thomas Jefferson once said that "difference of opinion leads to inquiry, and inquiry to truth." Jefferson, a broadly educated man, argued that "if a nation expects to be ignorant and free . . . it expects what never was and never will be." As individuals and as a nation, it is imperative that we consider the opinions of others and examine them with skill and discernment. The Opposing Viewpoints Series is intended to help readers achieve this goal.

David L. Bender and Bruno Leone,
Founders

Greenhaven Press anthologies primarily consist of previously published material taken from a variety of sources, including periodicals, books, scholarly journals, newspapers, government documents, and position papers from private and public organizations. These original sources are often edited for length and to ensure their accessibility for a young adult audience. The anthology editors also change the original titles of these works in order to clearly present the main thesis of each viewpoint and to explicitly indicate the opinion presented in the viewpoint. These alterations are made in consideration of both the reading and comprehension levels of a young adult audience. Every effort is made to ensure that Greenhaven Press accurately reflects the original intent of the authors included in this anthology.

Introduction

*"Family preservation services are an appropriate strategy
for enabling some children to safely remain with their
families while a crisis is being diffused."*
—*Michael Weber,* National Resource Center on Child
Sexual Abuse News, *March/April 1996*

*"If state agencies focus on preserving biological families, foster
kids will continue to be shuffled around in the system."*
—Minnesota Daily, *June 24, 1998*

On December 14, 1996, former president Bill Clinton in-
structed the secretary of health and human services to develop strategies to move children out of foster care and into
permanent homes. He set a goal to at least double the number of adoptions among foster care children in six years. In response to Clinton's instructions, the Department of Health
and Human Services (HHS) introduced the child welfare initiative known as Adoption 2002. This initiative was founded
on the belief that every child deserves a stable, safe, and nurturing home rather than temporary placement in foster care.

The most significant result of Adoption 2002 was the enactment of the Adoption and Safe Families Act of 1997
(ASFA). This law marks a shift away from the philosophy of
"family preservation," the belief that efforts should be made
to reunite abused or neglected children with their biological
parents, and toward "permanency planning." The objective
of permanency planning is to find permanent adoptive
homes for abused and neglected children as soon as possible.
Before the ASFA, the Adoption Assistance and Child Welfare Act of 1980 shaped American adoption policies. This
legislation emphasized family preservation and regarded
adoption as an action that took place after reasonable efforts
to reunify a family had failed. The term "reasonable efforts"
has come to describe programs designed to help disadvantaged or troubled parents take care of their children. These
include education, job training, substance abuse programs,

and counseling. Other efforts that promote family preservation include kinship care arrangements, in which a child's relatives are encouraged to become his or her legal guardians.

Architects of the ASFA claimed that the escalating number of children entering foster care highlighted the urgent need to place more of them into adoption. Furthermore, they maintained that unnecessary measures to preserve families had not only increased the number of children entering foster care, but had also extended their stays in the foster care system. At the time, the number of children in foster care had doubled in a decade, reaching 500,000. Responding to this trend, the ASFA implemented changes on a federal level that decreased efforts to reunify families and provided incentives for couples to adopt. For instance, child welfare agencies are no longer required to pursue "reasonable efforts" before terminating parental rights if the child was exposed to evidently extreme or life-threatening neglect or abuse.

Today, the impacts of Adoption 2002 and the alignment of adoption policies with permanency planning are evident nationwide. In 1996, approximately 28,000 children in the United States were adopted from foster care. In 1998, after the ASFA was initiated, the number rose to 36,000. The following year, 46,000 foster children were adopted, surpassing that year's goal of 41,000. So far, the HHS has awarded financial bonuses to forty-two states for increasing their adoption of foster care children.

Many adoption professionals and advocates praise the changes the ASFA brought to adoption laws and practices. Some proponents insist that expediting the adoption process protects the future of troubled and disadvantaged children. The Search Institute, a public policy research organization, reports that teenagers that were adopted at birth are more likely than children raised in their own birth families to live in two-parent, middle-class families. In addition, according to the institute, adopted children perform better academically than children who are raised by single parents or grandparents.

Others assert that strategies to reunify families are generally unsuccessful in attaining the goal of family stability. Conservative policy analyst Patrick F. Fagan states,

> Because of their own high costs . . . family preservation services cannot be sustained for long periods; and because of high demand, caseworkers move quickly to take care of the next family in crisis. This approach did succeed in stopping the removal of children from the home, but not necessarily in preserving them from further abuse. . . . In New York City alone, during the 12 months of 1992, 21 children were killed by a parent or mother's boyfriend after the Child Welfare Administration had intervened.

Although Fagan presents an extreme example, he communicates the growing concern among child welfare professionals that preserving biological relationships may come into conflict with the child's best interest.

However, there is opposition to the shift of adoption philosophy from family preservation to permanency planning. Proponents of family reunification contend that the inherent value of biological relationships must be protected. Adoption expert James L. Gritter says, "Biological connection is no trifle. It is inherently meaningful, never something to underestimate or take lightly." In addition, the Family Preservation Institute, an organization that develops family preservation services, contends that most children benefit from remaining with their biological families: "People of all ages can best develop, with few exceptions, by remaining with their family or relying on them as an important resource."

Perhaps the most vocal opponent of the ASFA is the National Coalition for Child Protection Reform (NCCPR), an organization that works ardently to preserve troubled families. The organization contends that when the ASFA was introduced, "the debate over 'reasonable efforts' had taken an Orwellian turn. Child savers began blaming it for their own failure to get children out of foster care." Moreover, the NCCPR suggests that "reasonable efforts" were prematurely dismissed because "agencies typically made little or no effort at all to keep families together."

In their mission to prove that "reasonable efforts" are effective, the NCCPR studied the Homebuilders Program. In this program, according to the NCCPR, the social worker "spends her or his time in the family's home, so she can see the family in action" and addresses "the problems the family identifies." Their underlying goal is to "combine traditional counseling and parent education with a strong emphasis on providing 'hard' services to ameliorate the worst aspects of poverty." The NCCPR claims that the Homebuilders Program works. For instance, the coalition reports that when the state of Michigan adopted programs based on the Homebuilders model, only two children died during the first two years and none thereafter. In contrast, the NCCPR contends that when Illinois discontinued family preservation efforts, five children died of abuse in foster care in one year.

The initiation of Adoption 2002, particularly the enactment of the ASFA, has brought the most significant change to U.S. adoption practices in nearly two decades. Supporters of the initiative claim that the ideas of kinship and family must be reevaluated to serve the needs of children and that the HHS was justified in reducing the preference for biological connections. Nonetheless, organizations such as the NCCPR assert that if services to reunify families are unsuccessful, it is because they are either poorly planned or terminated before families are given the chance to succeed. The coalition concludes that deserting "reasonable efforts" may lead to the systematic separation of many disadvantaged families. *Adoption: Opposing Viewpoints* explores this topic and other contemporary adoption issues in the following chapters: Should Adoption Be Encouraged? Whose Rights Should Be Protected in the Adoption Process? Are Some Adoptions More Problematic than Others? Should Adoption Policies Be Changed? Addressing these questions reveals the diverse views on how the needs of dependent children must be fulfilled.

CHAPTER 1

Should Adoption Be Encouraged?

Chapter Preface

Most women who place their children up for adoption come from disadvantaged populations. Unable or unprepared to take on parenthood or a growing family, some of these parents view placing a child for adoption as a commitment to the child's welfare. Unfortunately, many of those who choose to raise an unplanned child face exceptional difficulties. According to the Child Welfare League of America, as many as one out of five children currently living in foster care will not successfully rejoin their biological parents.

Detractors of adoption insist that terminating the biological relationship between mother and child has deleterious and lasting consequences. According to anti-adoption activist Joss Shawyer, "The shock experienced by new-born babies separated from their mothers . . . contributes towards the high rates of psychiatric disturbances found amongst adopted people." Other critics assert that most adoptions are not justified and could be prevented by increased efforts to preserve biological families. Family law attorney Nanette Schoor suggests that "help should take some form of 'family preservation' funding programs that assist families before their children are removed."

Advocates of adoption maintain that efforts to reunify families do not prioritize the needs of children. As an adult who grew up in an adoptive family, Anne-Mary F. Judge debates the importance of a child's biological relationships: "As a happily adopted person, I find it very sad that our legal system's current focus on the supposed superiority of biological parents over adopted ones is preventing children from experiencing the love of caring parents." Others agree that preserving children's biological ties, instead of placing them in adoptive homes, may compromise their well-being. Jean Bethke Elshtain, a professor of social and political ethics, contends that laws attempting to reunify families make it "very difficult to take children away from demonstrably abusive biological parents."

These views animate the discussions concerning adoption policies and practices in the following chapter, "Should Adoption Be Encouraged?"

1

"Adoption works, and . . . it is the best of the available alternatives for children who have been subjected to abuse or neglect."

Adoption Should Be Encouraged

Elizabeth Bartholet

Elizabeth Bartholet is a law professor at the Harvard Law School and has written numerous books addressing adoption, reproductive technology, and parenting. In the following viewpoint excerpted from her book *Nobody's Children: Abuse and Neglect, Foster Drift, and the Adoption Alternative*, she responds to the belief that adoption irreparably disrupts children's lives. She claims that adoption is the best alternative for troubled children who cannot return to their homes. Attempting to preserve biological families that are unstable, according to Bartholet, is harmful because it returns children to abusive homes and entraps them in the foster care system. Therefore, she contends that placing them in caring families should be prioritized over sustaining their biological ties.

As you read, consider the following questions:
1. How does the author support her view that placing children into adoptive families is not harmful?
2. What evidence does Bartholet cite to support her argument that there are enough prospective parents for children in foster care?
3. According to Bartholet, why does the public stigmatize adoption?

Excerpted from *Nobody's Children*, by Elizabeth Bartholet. Copyright © 1999 by Elizabeth Bartholet. Reprinted by permission of Beacon Press, Boston.

There is a lot of positive talk about adoption today, and some action. One can easily get the sense that a revolution is in the works. [Former president Bill Clinton] has announced his Adoption 2002 initiative, calling for a doubling in the number of children adopted out of foster care. Congress has passed within the space of just a few years several pieces of legislation designed to promote adoption. New federal laws ban racial barriers to adoption, limit the excesses of family-preservation policies, encourage child welfare agencies to move more children at earlier stages into adoptive homes, and encourage potential adoptive parents by giving them tax credits for adoption expenses. State and local leaders have initiated reforms to place renewed emphasis on children's safety and welfare, and to make adoption a higher policy priority. And in the last few years the number of adoptions has been rising, with some states showing dramatic increases.

Today's talk of adoption, and some new initiatives in the works, raise the hope that our society might be ready to make genuine changes in its child welfare system, taking adoption seriously for the first time as an option for children whose parents are not capable of parenting. But it will take a lot of work to turn that hope into reality.

Estimates indicate that as of 1998 roughly 110,000 children in foster care had been freed for adoption, or had an adoption plan—about 20 percent of those in out-of-home care. Fifty-nine percent of these children are African-American, 29 percent are white, 10 percent are Hispanic, and 2 percent are of other races or ethnicities. But the need for adoption cannot be measured by these numbers. Many children are being kept in their families and in foster care, and shuffled back and forth between the two, for whom adoption should be considered, but is not. The claim has been that adoption wouldn't be good for them—that children are almost always best off with their parents. The assumption has been that adoption wouldn't be possible anyway—that the homes just aren't there for the black children, the damaged children, and the older children that dominate the foster care population.

The evidence is clear that adoption works, and that it is the best of the available alternatives for children who have been subjected to abuse or neglect. This is true in terms of all the measures social scientists use to assess well-being, including measures of self-esteem and outcome measures related to later education, employment, crime and the like. It is also true in terms of abuse and neglect rates. Indeed, adopted children are less likely to suffer child abuse than is the norm in the general population of children raised by their biological parents.

© Kirk Anderson. Used with permission.

Family preservationists' claim that adoption harms children by depriving them of their family and roots relies on speculative theories that adoptees suffer from "genealogical bewilderment" and the like. But empirical studies that assess how carefully selected samples and control groups of children actually fare in life, based on all the measures of human well-being that social scientists have devised, reveal no damage suffered by virtue of transferring children from their biological parents to adoptive parents. Children adopted early in infancy do essentially as well, on measures of self-esteem, attachment, and performance, as children in the general population. These studies confirm that what is central to children's welfare is that they be placed in an appropriately nurturing permanent home as early in life as possible.

1. But can adoption work for today's foster care population? Adoption skeptics say no. They say that the children in foster care are too damaged, and many of them too old, for adoption to work. They point to the numbers who are born impaired by drugs and alcohol, the numbers who suffer from physical and mental disabilities, the numbers who have been subjected to extreme forms of abuse and neglect, and the numbers who are in their teens, having first suffered harm in their original homes, followed by many years adrift in the foster care system, or moving back and forth from foster homes to their homes of origin. They argue that while adoption might work for healthy infants, it can't work for these children. They note that significant numbers of adoptions from foster care "disrupt," with the children sent back from their adoptive homes into the foster care system. They claim that the only solutions for this damaged, older population of children lie in renewed emphasis on family preservation, on long-term foster care or guardianship, and on group or institutional homes.

But the evidence indicates that adoption can and does work for children who are damaged and for children who are older. These children do have extra-ordinary needs. Most of them are far more likely to find the extra-ordinary parenting they require to overcome their history and heal their injuries in the adoptive parent population than in the families that subjected them to abuse and neglect, or in temporary foster care, or in institutional care.

The Capacity to Heal

A significant percentage of today's foster care and group home population are infants, many of whom were born showing the effects of their mother's use of alcohol and drugs during pregnancy. Many were removed as a result of their parents' substance abuse and related maltreatment during the period soon after birth. Drug experts have been arguing for years that "crack babies" and other infants whose mothers used licit and illicit drugs during pregnancy have a variety of special needs requiring special care, but that with that care they can flourish. These experts have advocated vigorously against simply writing off this generation of children and have testified specifically to their adoptability.

Studies of children who have suffered enormous emotional damage as a result of abuse and neglect, or wartime atrocities, show that adoption has the capacity to help many such children heal and recover, so that they can lead essentially normal lives. Adoption critics point to the adoption disruption statistics, but given the damage that so many foster care children have suffered, the fact that only roughly 10 percent of the adoptions out of the foster care system disrupt should be seen as a mark of the success achieved in these adoptive relationships. Studies of special-needs adoptions generally show that these adoptive families form the same kind of loving, committed, and satisfying family relationships as those formed in other adoptive families.

It is true that some older children in foster care have developed meaningful ties with biological parents, but adoption need not destroy such ties. There is an increasing tendency toward openness in adoption which would allow children to gain the permanence and committed parenting of an adoptive family, while maintaining healthy links with their family of origin.

It is also true that adoption works better for children when they are placed in infancy and when they have not been horribly damaged by abuse and neglect, or by the inconsistency and uncertainty in parenting arrangements characteristic of foster care. Adoption studies regularly confirm that age at the time of placement is the key predictor for how well adopted children will do. This is no surprise. And it is obviously no argument for giving up on adoption as a solution for the foster care population. Adoption will still work better for most foster children than any other option, although it is undoubtedly true that some children are so damaged by the maltreatment they suffered or by their experience in the child welfare system that they have to be relegated to institutional care.

Abuse, Neglect, and Foster Drift

These adoption studies *are* an argument for moving children out of their biological homes and on to adoptive homes as soon as it is reasonably clear that they are not likely to receive the kind of care from their parents that they need to thrive. Delay in adoption may not necessarily permanently destroy children. But abuse and neglect combined with foster drift injure children in ways that not only cause suffering but also damage their life prospects, diminishing the chances for them to flourish in the way that children adopted as infants typically do flourish. All too many foster children today *are* older and *have* suffered damage, and *do* as a result have diminished life prospects even in adoption. But these are realities that are in our power to change.

2. But can adoptive families be found for today's foster care population?

Adoption skeptics say no. They argue that potential adoptive parents are limited in number and interested only in healthy infants, and that the whites who make up most of the adoptive parent pool are not interested in the nonwhite children who make up most of the foster care pool.

The reality is that we have done more to drive prospective parents away from the foster care system than to draw them in. We could expand the existing parent pool by recruiting broadly; now we recruit on the most limited basis. We could socialize prospective parents in ways that would open their minds to the idea of parenting children born to other parents and other racial groups, and children who have physical and mental disabilities; for the most part we now do just the opposite.

Skeptics talk as if the number of adoptive parents and the nature of their interests were fixed in stone. In fact the "demand" for adoption is extremely malleable. What exists today is a reality that our social policies have created. History demonstrates our power to reshape this reality. Prior to the mid-nineteenth century there was no apparent interest in adoption, because there was no legal mechanism enabling adoption. It took legislative and administrative action setting up an adoption system before adoptive parents could step forward, but now that such a system has been created we have well over 100,000 adoptions per year, more than half of which are adoptions by nonrelatives. Prior to World War II there was no apparent interest in international adoption, but now that systems have been set up enabling prospective parents to adopt children from abroad, many thousands of foreign children per year come into the United States to be adopted by U.S. citizens—15,774 in fiscal year 1998. Until a couple of decades ago, the only children considered adoptable were healthy infants. Now that efforts have been made to recruit parents for children with disabilities, there are waiting lists for Down's Syndrome children and for other children who used to be relegated to institutional care. Even children with extreme disabilities have been placed by child welfare agencies that have made the effort to reach out to locate and educate potential adopters. NACAC—the North American Council on Adoptable Children—says that *no child* in the foster care system should be considered unadoptable.

Potential Pool of Adoptive Parents

The potential pool of adoptive parents is enormous—it dwarfs the pool of waiting children. About 1.2 million women are infertile and 7.1 percent of married couples, or 2.1 million. The infertile are potentially a significant resource for children in need of homes, but at present only a limited number of them adopt. It is even more rare for the fertile to think of adoption as a way to build, or add to, their family. About 1 percent of women age 18–44, or 500,000 are currently seeking to adopt. Only 0.2 percent, or 100,000, had applied to an adoption agency. It is safe to assume that millions more would have pursued adoption had our social policies encouraged rather than discouraged them.

Ours is a society that glorifies reproduction, drives the infertile to pursue treatment at all costs, socializes them to think of adoption as a second-class form of parenting to be pursued only as a last resort, and regulates adoption in a way that makes it difficult, degrading, and expensive. We could instead encourage not only the infertile but the fertile to think of adoption as a normal way to build their families. We now ask young couples when they are going to have their first baby. We could ask them when they are thinking of expanding their family, and whether they are thinking about adoption or procreation or both. We could encourage all adult members of our society to think that their responsibility as members of the national community includes caring for the youngest members of that community when care is needed. . . .

Focus On Their Future

We know better than we do. We know that children require nurturing environments to thrive today and to have promising prospects for tomorrow. Common sense, confirmed by the research, tells us that children who are severely abused and neglected will do best if removed and placed permanently with families where they will receive the kind of nurturing likely to help them recover from their wounds. Common sense, confirmed by the research, tells us they would do better yet if we moved them when abuse and neglect were first manifest. This does not mean that in all cases of severe abuse and neglect we should immediately terminate the parents' rights and move children on to adoption. But it does mean that we should consider immediate termination of parental rights in many more cases and place a much higher priority on prompt adoptive placement.

We also know, or should know, that once we decide that children cannot be adequately nurtured in their homes of origin, they will be best off if we focus not simply on keeping them connected with their roots, but on taking care of them today in a way that will enable them to function tomorrow. Richard Barth, of the Jordan Institute for Families at the University of North Carolina School of Social Work, stands out as one of the few scholars willing to state the obvious: that for children to thrive it is important that we focus not just on their past but on their present and their future; that it matters if they are brought up by people who are capable of nurturing them, and in schools and communities where they can learn and be safe from violence.

> *"We must stop using the* permanent *practice of adoption to solve what are often* temporary *problems."*

Adoption Should Be Abolished

Evelyn Burns Robinson

In the following viewpoint, Evelyn Burns Robinson argues that adoption should be abolished because it is a punitive, permanent solution to the temporary challenges of unplanned parenthood. Convinced that adoption routinely separates disadvantaged families, she argues that support for struggling mothers should be increased to enable them to care for their children. Robinson is a former high school teacher and a social worker with the Association Representing Mothers Separated from their Children (ARMS) in Adelaide, South Australia. She is the author of *Adoption and Loss: The Hidden Grief,* in which she reflects upon her experiences as an adolescent mother who relinquished her first child.

As you read, consider the following questions:

1. According to Robinson, what "humane alternative" to adoption was recently considered by the New Zealand government?
2. Why is the grief of adoption experienced by a mother and her child inconsolable, in Robinson's opinion?
3. In the author's view, how can children who cannot remain with their birth parents be cared for?

There is no justification for adoption. Why do some governments persist in issuing adopted children with new birth certificates, which are a fabrication? It is offensive to natural mothers to find that both their existence and their experience are so easily obliterated with the stroke of a pen. Adopted people also object to their original details being officially erased. [Therapist Betty Jean] Lifton describes how, because of the fact that they are issued with a new birth certificate, adopted people grow up believing that their 'birth heritage is disposable.' [Feminist Joss] Shawyer describes the falsification of birth records as, 'an insult to personal dignity.'

Our moral awareness is continually growing. Policies and practices that once were acceptable are no longer tolerated. Slavery was legal in the United States until just over a hundred years ago. Now it is abhorred. In 1999, we are appalled to think that communities once bought and sold people, uprooting them from their families and transplanting them elsewhere. To us, it is clear that slavery is ethically wrong and morally indefensible. We wonder how apparently upright, moral people, such as ministers of religion, could not only defend but practise slavery, extolling its virtues. Slavery's defenders pointed out that slaves were better off being owned by a good master, that it provided them with a home and security and rescued them from a life of disadvantage. Slaves were expected to be grateful. It took a long time for these ideas to be challenged. Now we take for granted the basic human right of freedom, the respect for human dignity that does not allow trade in human beings. Why did people buy slaves? Because they wanted them and society said that they could.

In some countries, such as Australia, adoption is still legal. In some countries it has never existed and never will. In such places, people would react with horror to the very idea of permanently changing the parenthood and genealogy of a child. Adoption's defenders describe how adoption saves children from a lifetime of disadvantage, gives them security and a good home, for which they should be grateful. Does that sound familiar? Why did people adopt children? Because they wanted them and society said that they could.

It is time for society to realise that adoption is ethically wrong and morally indefensible. The idea that adoption is socially acceptable needs to be strenuously challenged. People need to be educated to see adoption for what it is, and to abandon it, in the same way that they had to be educated to denounce slavery.

Sadly, most academics who write about adoption take it as a given and do not question its existence. [Professor David] Howe et al, for example, write about, '. . . the conditions that make adoption necessary.' There are no conditions that make adoption necessary, because *adoption is not necessary* and it never has been necessary. Adoption was a social experiment. The tragic outcomes of this experiment make it clear that the way ahead must be a future without adoption. Robert Ludbrook, a lawyer and founding member of Jigsaw, presented an interesting paper at the Adoption and Healing Conference in New Zealand in 1997 entitled *Closing the Wound*, subtitled, *An Argument for the Abolition of Adoption*. In it he explains why he believes that, '. . . adoption no longer serves any overriding social purpose which outweighs its negative aspects.' At the time of writing this book, January 2000, the New Zealand government is considering the question of whether or not to abolish adoption and replace it with a system of "legal parenthood" which would convey the rights and responsibilities of parenthood without changing the child's identity and without involving secrecy and inaccessible records. It will be very interesting to see if New Zealand has the courage to take the lead in putting an end to adoption and putting the effort into creating a more humane alternative. ["Legal parenthood" was enacted that same year.]

Mothers grieve for the loss of their children and children grieve for the loss of their mothers. Natural mothers and adopted people deserve appropriate services to assist them to deal with their grief, but we must be very careful to distinguish between addressing the needs of those whose lives have already been affected by adoption and preventing further grief. There is no evidence, to my knowledge, that providing counselling before removing women's children from them will prevent them suffering from future grief reactions associated with the loss of those children. There is no "right" way to perform a permanent, legal separation of a mother from her child. Regardless of any counselling which occurs, these mothers will still have to deal with the fact that they have apparently voluntarily given away their children and that their children still exist and so their loss will never be final. Those mothers whose children are taken from them without their consent are still considered to be responsible, as the separation has apparently been caused by their failure to provide a safe home environment for their children. Neither is any amount of counselling for mothers at the time of separating them from their children going to help those children to come to terms with their loss. Mothers and children separated by adoption grieve because they have been separated. Extenuating factors exacerbate their grief, but the actual cause of the grief is the separation itself.

The Extended Family and Social Circle

There are certainly children, sadly, who are not safe with their natural families. How are we to care for them? A safe environment needs to be found for them, preferably with members of their extended family or social circle, in a situation with which they are already familiar. Family links should be maintained at all costs. There is never any need for a permanent, legal separation of parents and children. If there are children who are genuinely not safe growing up with their original families and find themselves growing up with those to whom they are not related, their original names and identities must be maintained. There must be no more pretence and denial. These children have a right to know who they are and to whom they are related.

Adoption has traditionally been used as a punishment for the parents, although welfare agencies would not admit to this. What they fail to realise is that this separation is also a punishment for the children. Separating parents from children does not teach the parents to modify their behaviour, nor does it offer them any hope or incentive to do so. It does not teach them parenting skills; it also does not prevent the parents from having more children. If our current foster care system is not serving children well, that is no excuse to continue to have them adopted. That is a reason to improve the service we can provide to children in need. The whole system of alternative care for children needs to be redesigned with the best interests of children in mind. We need to look closely at foster care and at guardianship so that we can provide what children need, whether it is short term or long term care. Our children deserve the best care that we can provide for them. I have great admiration for those who open their homes to children in need, expecting nothing in return but the satisfaction of knowing that they have made a difference. There is a trend in many countries now towards family preservation programmes, in which efforts are made to keep families together. Hopefully, these will gradually take the place of adoption policies, which actually cause family breakdown.

Severing the Connection

I believe that this connection [between mother and child], established during the nine months in utero, is a profound connection, and it is my hypothesis that the severing of that connection between the child and biological mother causes a primal or narcissistic wound which often manifests in a sense of loss (depression), basic mistrust (anxiety), emotional and/or behavioral problems and difficulties in relationships with significant others. I further believe that the awareness, whether conscious or unconscious, that the original separation was the result of relinquishment affects the adoptee's sense of Self, self-esteem and self-worth.

Nancy Verrier, *The Primal Wound: Legacy of the Adopted Child*, April 11, 1991.

There are some who say that children need the security of adoption. Children do, certainly, benefit from a feeling of security, but they do not necessarily obtain that from being adopted. In fact, it is not an adoption order that provides children with security. In many cases people adopt a child only to decide after some time that they no longer want the child. The child is then returned to the authorities, sometimes fostered, sometimes re-adopted. It is unconditional love that provides children with a feeling of security, not a piece of paper. Many children feel happy and secure living with people who are not their parents, regardless of whether they are adopted or not and, sadly, many children do not feel appreciated, nor secure, living with their natural or adoptive parents. Adoptive parents sometimes divorce and separate, they abuse and neglect their children, just as natural parents do. What children in need of care certainly do deserve is to maintain their identity and their links with their families and to grow up with honesty and openness. Our children and our families deserve the best possible service in times of crisis.

The Permanent Practice for Temporary Problems

There seems to be a growing emphasis, especially in the United States, on the provision of material possessions. Young women are still being pressured into giving away their children simply because they are in a disadvantaged position (which is probably temporary) financially. This emphasis is quite inappropriate and very saddening. A sense of belonging and of being valued cannot be bought. I am sure that if a random sample of the adult population was questioned about their fondest childhood memories, very few of them would mention the amount of money that was spent on them. Children and their parents should only be separated when there is an issue of the child's safety, not ever simply because someone else is in a position to spend more money on that child.

Women must stop taking other women's children. If a woman is unable to care for her child because she lacks the skills, then we should try to teach her the skills. If a woman is temporarily in a situation that would be unsafe for her child, then by all means care for the child elsewhere, but in the meantime help the woman to get out of her dangerous situation. If poverty is the issue, then strategies need to be put in place to address the poverty. Women in trouble need support. They do not need to be made to feel even more powerless by being robbed of their children. We must stop using the *permanent* practice of adoption to solve what are often *temporary* problems. If there is a permanently unsuitable situation, for example where the mother suffers from a mental health problem which would put her child at risk, then we should arrange for the child to be cared for elsewhere, but should not abandon and punish the mother. Both mother and child will benefit from enjoying an on-going, if necessary supervised, relationship. There is no justification in such cases for changing the child's identity and pretending that the child has a different mother. If a woman wishes to have a child and is unable to, she has no right to take a child from another woman to fulfil her desire. Adoption is largely a women's issue as women are the ones who bear children. Men, unfortunately, are most often the ones who make adoption policies. Women must make their voices heard and force changes to outdated adoption policies. . . .

For each adoption that takes place, many people are affected. Each adopted person has four parents, they may have siblings in their adoptive family and siblings in their natural family (say two of each), they may have a partner themselves and children of their own, perhaps two. This makes an average of twelve people directly affected by each adoption, before we even consider grandparents and other extended family members. In the United States it has been estimated that there are currently six million adopted people. World-wide, there is a vast number of people whose lives have been directly affected by adoption. These are the casualties of adoption. At the International Conference on Adoption and Healing held in New Zealand in 1997, Keith Griffith said, 'Healing needs to be more than running an ambulance at the bottom of the cliff. It must also demand the removal of factors that push people over the top.'

Perhaps now we can all recognise that those whose lives have been affected by adoption have been damaged by the experience and are entitled to assistance and support. It is time for society to acknowledge that the grief of those who have been separated by adoption is legitimate and is, in fact, the appropriate, expected response to their experiences. Hopefully the community in general will now realise that family members who have been separated by adoption are still family members and that it is natural and commendable for them to wish to know each other. Let us hope that we can look forward to a more enlightened future, where parents are supported to raise their own children and where everyone recognises that it is wrong to take another person's child, no matter what the circumstances.

"Adoption . . . is altruistic—life for a child and a gift to an often-childless couple."

Adoption Is an Alternative to Abortion and Single Parenting

Marvin Olasky

In the following viewpoint, Marvin Olasky claims that adoption is the best choice for unmarried pregnant women instead of abortion or single parenting. Abortion harms women and unborn children, Olasky claims, and placing single mothers on welfare cannot provide children with the stable environment they need. He argues making the adoption process easier for couples who wish to adopt would help to deter abortion, place children in stable, two-parent homes, and reduce federal spending on welfare. Olasky is the editor of *World* magazine, has written numerous books endorsing conservative public policies, and is a longtime adviser to forty-third president George W. Bush.

As you read, consider the following questions:
1. How does the author support his claim that the media's perception of adoption is biased?
2. According to Olasky, what proportion of unmarried pregnant women choose adoption?
3. In Olasky's view, what are the four ways adoption can be transformed into a popular choice?

Reprinted, with permission, from Marvin Olasky, "Forgotten Choice: Adoption Is a Rebuke to Abortion and Single-Parenting, and the Liberal Media Will Have None of It," *National Review*, March 10, 1997; © 1997 by National Review, Inc., 215 Lexington Ave., New York, NY 10016.

S chizophrenia, thy name is adoption! Here are some of adoption's multiple personalities, as judged by media depictions [in recent] years:

- Polls show adoption in the abstract to be almost as popular as motherhood itself, but some leaders in media and academia still pin a scarlet letter on adoptees.
- *New York Times* editors who automatically delete demeaning references to minorities or women allowed one reporter to emphasize that an alleged multiple murderer was adopted: "Though experts were careful to say that adoption was no indicator of criminal tendencies, they noted that a number of serial killers like David Berkowitz, Son of Sam, had been adopted."
- Studies conducted by the Search Institute and other organizations show adolescents adopted as infants doing as well psychologically as their non-adopted peers, but critics of adoption proclaim that every adopted baby has experienced a "primal wound" that can lead to extreme behavior. . . .
- Although most adoptions work out very well, television's sewer talk shows feature not only freaky perversions but tortured birthmothers describing their regrets about placing children for adoption years before, and teary teens describing their desperate efforts to locate birthmothers who preferred to remain hidden.

Impressions from such shows, along with those left by all the tug-of-war stories about Baby Jessica and Baby Richard, lead to a typical teen perspective described by Mary Beth Style, formerly of the National Council for Adoption: "They think it inevitable that they'll change their minds, that there will be a battle, or that they'll be miserable their whole lives if they place for adoption." [In the mid-1990s, children known as "Jessica" and "Richard," raised in adoptive homes since their births, were controversially returned to their birthparents by the courts.]

Barriers to Adoption

That perception forms the biggest barrier to adoption today. Adoption is popular in opinion polls and among politicians who can gain the benefits of baby-kissing without the danger of infant counterattack via spit-up. Adoption also has become a way for some proponents of abortion to retract their horns and suggest that they do feel others' pain; Hillary Clinton mused about her desire to adopt, someday, and one of her newspaper columns noted that she and Mother Teresa "differ on some issues" but agree on the need to promote adoption.

Adoption is unpopular, however, among those who are the decision-makers: fewer than 2 of every 100 unmarried pregnant women choose adoption. The enemies of adoption are single-parenting, which still receives special economic support via the welfare system, and abortion, which receives special legal privileges through judicial fiat. Adoption is squeezed out.

Most attempts to spur adoption so far have been either inconsequential or even counter-productive. During [recent] years "National Adoption Month" (November) and "National Adoption Week" (around Thanksgiving time) produced not much more than some cute human-interest features, such as those depicting "adoption fairs" in which older children messed up by foster care are paraded before potentially welcoming adults. Such events may help some children to find homes, but what does a teen mom think when she sees children displayed—"Check their teeth, honey"—in this way? . . .

Let's get serious—and getting serious first means defining the problem correctly. The new adoption tax credit for adoptive families is good and fair, but the main adoption bottleneck is not a lack of potential adoptive families. Two million couples are waiting to adopt, and infants of every skin color or level of disability can be placed.

The key problem is the supposed superiority of the two major alternatives to adoption. Abortion seems to convey an immediate benefit: It makes the problem disappear. (And don't worry about death or post-abortion regrets that may grow more severe as time goes by.) Despite 1996's welfare-reform bill, single-parenting still conveys benefits. Adoption, on the other hand, is altruistic—life for a child and a gift to an often-childless couple—but it is also inconvenient and embarrassing, especially when compared to abortions done in secret. Teenagers generally ask not what they can do for others, but what others are thinking about them. Is it any surprise that adoption is usually ignored?

Until thirty years ago the better options for unmarried pregnant women—marriage and adoption—held their own. From 1965 to 1973, however, Washington overrode state and local preferences and installed a bad choice, single-parenting, as a fundamental economic right, and a homicidal choice, abortion, as a fundamental legal right. Those preferences are still largely in effect, even though numerous research studies show that single-parenting is socially, economically, and psychologically destructive, but adoption of infants overwhelmingly works out well for babies, birthparents, and adoptive parents.

Giving Adoption a Fair Chance

It is time, therefore, to look at four ways to give adoption once again a fair chance to increase its popularity among the young decision-makers:

First, in the short run, compensate (slightly) for governmental support of the two bad alternatives by providing governmental support for the two good alternatives. As long as governmental welfare still plagues the poor, at least it should promote marriage ("wedfare") rather than discourage it. Another discerning approach is that pushed forward by Sen. Dan Coats (R., Ind.) and Rep. Chris Smith (R., N.J.). They have introduced legislation to provide pregnant women with vouchers for maternity home services.

Such legislation would lead to more women entering maternity homes and more adoptions. Young women in such homes typically take classes concerning all their options instead of reacting to single-parenting pressures from friends. For example, 230 out of 575 babies born at a ten-year-old Kansas City maternity home known as The Light House—40 per cent—have been placed for adoption.

Second, the long run goal should be to eliminate support for the bad alternatives. Instead of constantly raising the bridge by expanding government, lower the river. Replacing the welfare system with community-based approaches is essential. Adoption will be aided further if we defund Planned Parenthood, pass parental-consent laws and other protective devices for unborn children, and eventually add to the Constitution a pro-life amendment.

Opposing bad choices in the culture generally also is vital. If the belated liberal criticism of single-parenting that has become common in recent years is combined with the belated liberal questioning of abortion that has recently emerged, adoption becomes the logical alternative. All cannot be sweetness and light; for adoption to flourish, the other alternatives need to become shameful once again.

Third, we can transform the system as it affects older children by eliminating the incentives to shuttle them from foster-care home to foster-care home and rip their hearts out in the process. No child likes to think that he may be here today, gone tomorrow, but close to 100,000 children have flopped around in foster care for over seven years. A $10-billion foster-care industry created and supported by government allows administrators and social workers to feather their own nests as they keep children from having one of their own. The financial incentive for government bureaucrats is to maintain children in foster care; managers who place all of their charges in permanent homes lose funding.

Benefiting Birth Mothers

Adoption benefits *birth mothers*. A study done by the Search Institute found that a young woman who makes an adoption plan is less likely to be on welfare. Less likely to find herself in another out-of-wedlock pregnancy. And more likely to finish school and find a steady job.

Rosaline Bush, *Family Voice*, January 1997.

Young people can be saved physically and emotionally if parents who abandon or repeatedly abuse their children face termination of parental rights in six months, and the children then are placed in permanent adoptive homes within thirty days following termination. That is doable as long as there is zero toleration of adoption delays because of race or ethnicity. There are plenty of adoptive homes for children up through age seven; only after that, when children have been in foster care for years and suffered emotional lynching in the process, does placement become sticky.

Fourth, we should transcend the current system by radical deregulation of the entire infant adoption process. While hundreds of thousands of women have abortionists kill unborn children who are half a year short of birth, hundreds of thousands of husbands and wives who want to adopt a child are frustrated. Markets exist to bring together buyers and sellers; one reason for America's 1.5 million abortions each year is a refusal to let the market work in this situation, due to legitimate concerns about baby-selling and racism.

Slash Through the Red Tape

Why not slash through the red tape and allow adoptive parents (without criminal records) and birth parents (with ample counseling) to arrive at arrangements they choose? Problems evidently will emerge, but joys far greater will abound. Why not get government out of adoption entirely by privatizing adoption services so that children who are abandoned or abused come under the care of particular religious or community organizations that are willing to serve them, rather than becoming wards of the state? Why not stipulate that a mother who produces a cocaine-addicted baby is by definition an unfit mother?

Examination of these and other questions will push political leaders far beyond the relatively easy matter of tax credits, and journalists beyond the easy feature stories about adoption fairs. To put hard questions about hard lives on the front page, a congressional-appointed national commission on adoption and foster care would be useful.

> *"Promoting adoption instead of abortion sounds life-affirming, but it's actually physically dangerous, cruel and punitive."*

Adoption Is Not an Alternative to Abortion

Katha Pollitt

Katha Pollitt is an associate editor and columnist for the *Nation*, a journal of progressive opinion, and author of *Reasonable Creatures: Essays on Women and Feminism*. In the following viewpoint, Pollitt asserts that adoption cannot serve as an alternative to abortion. She claims that preventing a woman from terminating her pregnancy is traumatic and dangerous because giving birth to a child has lasting physical, emotional, and social effects upon the mother. Furthermore, adoption should not be promoted as a solution to poverty and unplanned parenthood. Instead of encouraging adoption, Pollitt insists that the United States should follow the lead of similar countries and promote sex education and contraception and provide economic assistance to poor single mothers.

As you read, consider the following questions:
1. How does the author support her view that there may not be enough potential adoptive parents to make increasing adoption successful?
2. What is the author's opinion of open adoptions?
3. According to Pollitt, how was adoption encouraged in the 1950s and 1960s?

Reprinted, with permission, from Katha Pollitt, "Adoption Fantasy," *The Nation*, July 8, 1996.

Bill Clinton loves it. Bob Dole, too. Newt Gingrich thinks it's so terrific he wanted to mass-produce it through the Personal Responsibility Act. Hillary Clinton told *Time* she dreamed of trying it herself. As the "family values"/teen-sex/abortion debate winds on with no end in sight, adoption is being touted as a rare area of consensus: the way to discourage "illegitimacy" while providing poor children with stable homes, the peace pipe in the abortion wars. Whatever may be the difficulties and conflicts of actual people involved in the adoption triangle, at the political level, it's all win-win: adoption and apple pie.

Whenever I question the facile promotion of adoption as a solution to the problem du jour I get angry letters from adoptive parents. So I want to be clear: Of course adoption can be a wonderful thing; of course the ties between adoptive parents and children are as profound as those between biological ones. But can't one both rejoice in the happiness adoption can bring to individuals and ask hard questions about the social functions it is being asked to fill? I can't be the only person who has noticed that the same Administration that supports the family cap—the denial of a modest benefit increase to women who conceive an additional child while on welfare—is about to bestow on all but the richest families a $5,000 tax credit to defray the costs of adoption. Thus, the New Jersey baby who is deemed unworthy of $64 a month, or $768 a year, in government support if he stays in his family of origin immediately becomes six times more valuable once he joins a supposedly better-ordered household. Maybe unwed mothers should trade kids.

The "Alternative" to Abortion

Mass adoption was supposed to rescue innocent babies from the effects of defunding their guilty teenage mothers—a bizarre brainstorm of Charles Murray that has fortunately faded for now. [Now], adoption is back in a more accustomed role, as an "alternative" to abortion—a notion long supported by abortion-rights opponents from Ralph Reed to Christopher Hitchens, and recently picked up by some pro-choicers too. The wrong women insisting on their right to have children, the right women refusing to—it's hard to avoid the conclusion that as public policy, adoption is being pushed as a way of avoiding hard questions about class and sex. After all, if poverty is the problem, we could enable mothers and children to live decently, as is done throughout Western Europe. If teenage pregnancy is the problem, we could insist on contraception, sex education and health care—the approach that has also worked very well in Western Europe, where teens are about as sexually active as they are in this country, but where rates of teen pregnancy range from half of ours (England and Wales) to one-tenth (the Netherlands).

A Basic Fundamental Right

If you're forcing somebody to have a baby, making a lifetime decision against their will, then problems are going to turn up and they're not going to be very happy about that. They're probably going to be extremely depressed.

I feel abortion is a part of life. Having a child or not having a child is a basic fundamental right for men and women. The size of one's family is a basic fundamental right. I could just as easily work in a fertility clinic as an abortion clinic, or in an adoption agency, because it is all part of the rich texture of people's lives. That they are able to choose what they want to do. I don't see it as any different.

Anonymous, interviewed by Patricia Lunneburg, *Abortion: A Positive Decision*, 1992.

How much sense does adoption make as a large-scale alternative to abortion? Journalists constantly cite the National Council for Adoption's claim that 1–2 million Americans wish to adopt—which would make between twenty and forty potential adopters for every one of the 50,000 or so non-kin adoptions formalized in a typical year. But what is this estimate based on? According to the N.C.A., it's a rough extrapolation from figures on infertility, and includes anyone who makes any gesture in the direction of adoption—even a phone call—which means they are counting most of my women friends, some of the men and, who knows, may be Hillary Clinton too. The number of serious, viable candidates is bound to be much smaller: For all the publicity surrounding their tragic circumstances, in 1995 Americans adopted only

2,193 Chinese baby girls. Even if there were no other objections, the adoption and abortion numbers are too incommensurate for the former to be a real "alternative" to the latter.

But of course, there are other objections. There are good reasons why only 3 percent of white girls and 1 percent of black girls—and an even tinier percentage of adult women—choose adoption. Maybe more would do so if adoption were more fluid and open—a kind of open-ended "guardianship" arrangement—but that would surely discourage potential adoptive parents. The glory days of white-baby relinquishment in the 1950s and 1960s depended on coercion—the illegality of abortion, the sexual double standard and the stigma of unwed motherhood, enforced by family, neighbors, school, social work, medicine, church, law. Those girls gave up their babies because they had no choice—that's why we are now hearing from so many sad and furious 50-year-old birth mothers. Do we really want to create a new generation of them by applying the guilt and pressure tactics that a behavior change of such magnitude would require?

Cruel and Punitive

Right now, pregnant girls and women are free to make an adoption plan, and for some it may indeed be the right choice. But why persuade more to—unless one espouses the anti-choice philosophy that even the fertilized egg has a right to be born, and that terminating a pregnancy is "selfish"? I'm not belittling the longings of would-be adoptive parents, but theirs is not a problem a teenager should be asked to solve. Pregnancy and childbirth are immense events, physically, emotionally, socially, with lifelong effects; it isn't selfish to say no to them.

Promoting adoption instead of abortion sounds life-affirming, but it's actually physically dangerous, cruel and punitive. That's why the political and media figures now supporting it wouldn't dream of urging it on their own daughters. Can you imagine the Clintons putting Chelsea through such an ordeal? Hillary Clinton is entitled to her adoption fantasy, but maybe she ought to think a little more about the girls who are already here. They have a right to put themselves first.

Periodical Bibliography

The following articles have been selected to supplement the diverse views presented in this chapter. Addresses are provided for periodicals not indexed in the *Readers' Guide to Periodical Literature*, the *Alternative Press Index*, the *Social Sciences Index*, or the *Index to Legal Periodicals and Books*.

Lori B. Andrews	"When Baby Makes More Than Three," *Washington Post*, May 10, 1999.
Laura Byrd	"Life and Ideals: The Lost Ones," *World and I*, June 1999. Available from 3600 New York Ave. NE, Washington, DC 20002.
Hillary R. Clinton	"Every Child Deserves a Caring Family," *Liberal Opinion Week*, December 7, 1998. Available from PO Box 880, First Ave., Vinton, IA 52349-0880.
Madelyn Freundlich	"Adoption Ambivalence," *Children's Voice*, Spring 1998. Available from the Child Welfare League of America, 440 First St. NW, 3rd Floor, Washington, DC 20001-2085.
Olivia Gans and Mary Spaulding Balch	"Argument 3: 'Every Child a Wanted Child' and Other Social Arguments," *National Right to Life News*, April 14, 1998. Available from the National Right to Life Committee, 419 7th St. NW Suite 500, Washington, DC 20004.
Derek Herbert	"Too Many Kids Waiting for a Home," *Washington Times*, May 14, 1997.
Albert R. Hunt	"A National Dialogue to Build on Adoption Progress," *Wall Street Journal*, November 19, 1999.
Warren Johnson	"A Much Broader Definition of the Label 'Pro-life,'" *San Diego Union-Tribune*, February 9, 1997.
Tamar Levin	"Alumni Fight for Soul of Richest Orphanage," *New York Times*, November 30, 2000.
K. Mahler	"Young Mothers Who Choose Adoption May Be Regretful, But Not Usually Depressed," *Family Planning Perspectives*, May/June 1997. Available from the Alan Guttmacher Institute, 120 Wall St., 21st Floor, New York, NY 10005.
Richard C. Paddock	"The Grim Face of Russia's Orphanages," *Los Angeles Times*, November 17, 1998.

CHAPTER 2

Whose Rights Should Be Protected in the Adoption Process?

Chapter Preface

Although the biological father may consent to adoption at any time during a pregnancy, the biological mother must give birth before she executes her consent (except in Alabama and Hawaii). Forty-six states and the District of Columbia have statutes that specify the length of time that birth mothers must wait before consenting to an adoption. The minimum waiting period ranges from twelve hours to three days after giving birth.

Since adoption is intended to place children in stable, permanent homes, a valid consent to adoption is considered irrevocable. However, to safeguard birth parents from making hasty, regrettable decisions, a period is observed in which a consent to adoption may be retracted. Although the time period varies from state to state, generally a consent can be retracted within twenty-one days.

Some adoption experts and activists favor extending the period of time in which birth parents may revoke a consent to adoption. They argue that adoption is a formidable, lasting decision and that the emotional turbulence caused by pregnancy, childbirth, and the influence of the prospective adoptive parents may impair the birth parents' judgment. According to attorney Carole Anderson, "No one can know what it is like to be a parent until the baby arrives. No doubt that is why those who promote family separation also push for early surrenders."

However, detractors insist that lengthening the period of revocation will exacerbate the burden of an adoption decision upon the birth parents. Adoption professional Mary Beth Style asserts that "human beings can only handle the emotional intensity of a crisis for a limited amount of time." If adoption crises are prolonged, she argues, "women may be making decisions just to get the decision over with."

The issue of consent raises questions of how to balance the rights of the birth parents, adoptive parents, and the child in the adoption process. Experts and activists attempt to clarify these rights in the following chapter.

"*A potential birthmother does not need to be thinking about the plight of childless couples.*"

The Rights of Birth Mothers Must Be Protected

Heather Lowe

The biological mother of an adopted child is commonly referred to as the "birth mother." In the following viewpoint, Heather Lowe argues that as the adoption industry becomes increasingly profitable, the rights of birth mothers must be protected. Prospective birth mothers are typically uninformed of all their options, rights, and the risks of adoption, Lowe asserts. Many are pressured to terminate their parental rights by child placement professionals who are motivated by personal bias or financial gain. Therefore, she urges that numerous adoption reforms be implemented to protect birth mothers' rights and their biological ties to their children. Lowe is a writer and editor for a forestry company in Summerville, South Carolina. As a birth mother and adoption reform activist, she volunteers with Concerned United Birthparents, an organization dedicated to preventing unnecessary adoptions and supporting birth parents' rights.

As you read, consider the following questions:
1. In the author's opinion, what is the status of birth mothers?
2. According to Lowe, why should adoptive parents be kept out of the delivery room and hospital during the birth?
3. Why does Lowe oppose closed adoptions?

Reprinted, with permission, from Heather Lowe, "A Birthmother's View of Adoption: Suggestions for Reform," article found at www.adopting.org/BirthmothersViewOfAdoption.html.

When my son made his entrance into the world in November 1998, a second birth took place. There on the delivery table, soaked in sweat and blood, I was reborn as a birthmother. In the long days since that double birth, I have grieved a grief of a severity I didn't think possible. I have reached new depths of suffering, and I have lived the meaning of regret. For a person who despises victimhood and espouses personal responsibility, this has been a hard role to accept—but the truth remains . . . I was hurt by bad laws.

The Birthmother Status

No little girl grows up dreaming of becoming a birthmother; a role that is generally either ignored or despised. Yet millions of women carry the badge. Increasingly we are more forthright about our aborted chance at motherhood, and some of us are even militant. . . .

Open adoption, in which adoptive families maintain ongoing, lifelong relationships with the birthfamily, has elevated birthmother status in important ways, but injustice in adoption remains rampant, and prejudices still abound. Would-be adopters and social workers alike have an image of the "typical" birthmother, and they look down on her in smug condescension. They think they are rescuing the poor confused dear, and expect her to be grateful to their charity in "saving" her child from a life that is not solidly middle class, or a home that is not two-parent.

Even after two decades of progress toward open adoption, birthmothers still pay. We pay every time someone tells us our child is so lucky to have found a good family (i.e., to be away from us?). We pay when coworkers (usually the same ones who told us during our pregnancies that it would be selfish to keep our children) go on to ask in disbelief, "How could you have given away your baby?" We pay dearly on Mother's Day, and we pay each time we are asked, "Do you have any children?"

I am not anti-adoption. Many cases really do call for a good adoptive family, and many children benefit from growing up outside their biological homes. But adoption as it is practiced today is a disgrace. It's become an industry geared not toward "the best interests of the child" (itself a worn out catchphrase with little real meaning) but toward serving people who think they have a God-given right to add a child to their home. Adoption used to be about finding homes for children, but now it's about finding children to fill the homes of infertile couples. To save the institution of adoption, I propose a list of nine reforms.

One Major Loss for Another

To understand why I make them, however, it's first necessary to have some background on me. For starters, I fit none of the birthmother stereotypes. Aged 27 when I gave birth, I was hardly a teen mother. I am not poor or unstable; I have a good job with a major corporation. I am not uneducated; I have a sharp mind and an undying love of learning. My child was unplanned, but not unwanted. My family and I had much to offer my son, save the one thing we could not give him: a father who stuck around.

Research into the effects of adoption on infants shows that the psychological cost of infant-maternal separation is so high that an adoption should only be done as a last resort. It is a well-documented fact that infants do suffer lifelong consequences as a result of separation from their first family, regardless of how joyous and successful their adoption eventually turns out to be. Experts in the field caution, therefore, that adoption should be done only if there is no other way for mother and baby to stay together. Unfortunately, this is not how adoption is commonly practiced. Agencies and private adoption "facilitators," which profit based on how many adoptions they can arrange, don't ask too many questions about why a potential birthmother is considering adoption.

So despite the red flags that the demographic indicators ought to have raised in my case, the adoption industry forged ahead, desperate to get one more healthy, white newborn. No one said to me, "If anyone has the resources to be a single parent, it's you." No one asked me why I was really choosing adoption, or if I was being influenced by those around me instead of going with my gut feelings. No one acknowledged that what I was actually trying to do was pay for my "sin" in getting pregnant out of wedlock—trying to make atonement by making an infertile married couple happy. The "counseling" I got was perfunctory and biased and all-around unacceptable (I'll have more to say about that in a moment.) But I didn't know better. Despite attacking the potential adoption of my son as a research project, and reading a great deal of material while pregnant, I did not collect enough unbiased information to fully understand what I was doing. No one knows just how to go about becoming a birthmother until it's already too late.

So, I signed the papers and they got the baby. But is this the basis for building a family—on the grief and regret of another? I often wonder how adoptive parents live with themselves, knowing how much they have taken away from my child's birthfamily. Unless, that is, it's absolutely clear that they are offering the child much more than the birthfamily could have done. My situation lacks such clarity. It is far too ambiguous. I fear that in the life of my son, I merely replaced one major loss (lack of a present father) with another (being cut out of his biological family).

Proposed Reforms

1. Eliminate biased social workers. When I was trying to decide if I was going to surrender my child to adoption, the agency provided the prospective adopters with a counselor, as well as one for me. But that counselor was herself an adoptive mother. In our "talks," she bubbled inanely about what a wonderful gift her daughter has been (as if the girl's birthmother had searched valiantly for the perfect present and done so much better than a gift certificate). Birthmothers do not give their children as gifts to needy parents; if anything they give the parents as gifts to their children.

This phenomenon of presenting adoption as "gift-giving" is far too prevalent. A potential birthmother does not need to be thinking about the plight of childless couples, no matter how sad infertility may be. A woman in the midst of a crisis pregnancy has been stigmatized as a bad girl, often experiencing the disapproval of and anger from family and friends. In order to regain her "good girl" status, she will do anything to make these people happy again, and giving away her baby to a needy couple seems like the perfect way out. The danger is that she will make an adoption decision based solely on the feelings of others. . . .

2. Mandate counseling for all potential birthmothers. Even if the expectant mother is in denial and thinks she does not need counseling, she is wrong. The law should require that she receive free counsel from an uninterested, outside party. Voluntarily losing one's child is the most serious loss most women will ever face. Being forced to do so without extensive advisement is sheer cruelty. . . .

The Biological Connection

Sociobiologists offer an interesting perspective on the vitality of the biological connection. They believe in a form of evolutionary programming—*kinship selection* or *inclusive fitness*, in their words—that moves people to favor relatives in the distribution of scarce resources. They suggest that this process of preferential sharing is ingrained in the human psyche to ensure nothing less than the survival of the species.

Though we struggle to find adequate words, there is something undeniably primal, powerful, and pleasing about swimming in a shared gene pool, and there is something visceral about automatic, presumptive, no-holds-barred identification with "one's own." Biological relatedness surely does not guarantee interpersonal harmony, but it is a formidable given in each person's life.

James L. Gritter, *Lifegivers: Framing the Birthparent Experience in Open Adoption*, 2000.

---

3. Train all hospital workers in sensitive adoption practices. The horror stories I have collected from other birthmoms regarding their experiences in the hospital are hair-curling, and they come from both sides of the fence. Every day I hear of nurses who think adoption is wrong and try to talk the birthmother into keeping the child in the biological family, or nurses who think adoption is glorious but that the birthmother is sinful and has no right to enjoy her own birthing. Both are equally offensive and could be cured with more education among hospital staff, who need to learn that their role is to make a mother's delivery as pleasant and stress-free as possible, regardless of what plans she may be making for her child. Doctors, nurses, and support staff should never express their opinions on the adoption plans taking place. In the meantime, potential birthmothers must take full control of their hospital experience and not let outside ignorance alter a well-made birthing plan.

4. Keep adoptive parents out of the delivery room and away from the hospital. They don't belong anywhere near the scene. This is hard for me to say, because my child's parents were in the delivery room (at their request, not mine) and it seemed at the time to be a relatively pleasant experience, though not without a measure of awkwardness. Looking back, however, I see how it interfered with my decision-making ability. Since then I've also learned more about the pre and perinatal experience of the child. The question ought to be, "Who does the adoptee want in the delivery room?" Unfortunately, this question is almost never asked.

According to psychologists, the newborn baby recognizes its mother immediately at birth. That baby needs time to continue the bond with his first mother, whom he already knows from forty weeks of sharing her body. The prospective adoptive mother, no matter how wonderful she may be, is still a stranger to the newborn, who does not experience himself as separate from his biological mother until the age of two months. There will be time for gentle transitions into an adoptive family later, if they are in fact needed.

Adoptions are often handled as if the baby is not really present. The thinking seems to be that if the switch-off is handled quickly enough, the baby will never notice. This is patently untrue, and rushing to place a child in an adoptive home does lasting damage.

There is yet another reason prospective adopters don't belong anywhere near a delivery room. No matter how much thought has gone into a pre-birth decision, an adoption plan must be made anew after the birth, once the child has become a reality. A great majority of first-time mothers report feeling disconnected from their child while pregnant—and these are women who planned their pregnancies and intend to keep their children. For most potential birthmothers, this is their first child, and they have no idea how they will feel after the baby's actual arrival. A child that they wonder if they could love is now known to be the most precious thing on earth to them. Yet adoption laws are mostly written by men, who have no idea that motherhood is a great unknown until it actually happens. We frequently hear about the horrible birthmother who so inconsiderately changes her mind, as if a change of heart is a sin. Yes, the prospective parents will face real pain if the birthmother decides to keep her baby. But the cold truth is that no one is going to leave that hospital without pain. The potential birthmother is expected to bear the pain, and to bear it FOREVER. When she backs away from that pain, she is treated as if she has violated a contract, much as if she were selling a car, not relinquishing a child. Most states do not allow an intent to relinquish statement, but those that do must act at once to outlaw them. . . .

5. *Abolish irrevocable consent.* Many states allow a window of time for birthmothers to change their minds about this most immense of decisions, but many do not. In addition, many states allow consents to be taken in a hospital bed, shortly after birth, rather than in a courtroom in front of a judge—the proper place for a decision of such solemnity to be formalized.

Imagine you are given 72 hours to decide whether you will lose your child. Is that enough time? The place you are given to do it is a hospital bed, where you lie worn out from labor, hovered over by anxious adoptive parents and their guests. Their joy at the new arrival is infectious, and you might start to think that life as a birthmother will always be this saturated in gratitude and happiness. Is that the proper atmosphere to make a decision which will completely recreate you as a person and affect the rest of your days? In three months, many things can change in a birthmom's life, factors that will make her want to keep her child. Give her the time and the space to make the decision, and if her economic or social standing has not improved or if she still doubts her mothering ability, proceed with the adoption.

6. *End adoption advertising.* Adoptive families like to say their families were formed by God. If so, then why do they need marketing to get the job done? If God wants to form a family by adoption, then prospective adoptive parents need to sit back, shut up and let Him do it. They shouldn't sell themselves with saccharine ads and gooey posters, troll for babies on the Internet, or omit crucial facts in those "Dear

Birthmother" letters. (And while they're at it, they should never refer to a pregnant woman as a "birthmother" at all. A woman is not a birthmother until she has signed away her legal rights to her child, so an expectant mother can never be a birthmother. Calling her one denies reality, forces her to think of herself as something she may not want to become, and is coercive in the extreme.) . . .

There are plenty of non-coercive, dignified ways for prospective adopters to get the word out that they hope to adopt. Let's use them. We must bring back integrity to the adoption process. . . .

7. *Let closed adoptions dwindle like the Dark Age remnant they are.* I have no respect for potential adoptive families who would even consider a closed adoption. Adoptive parents in a closed adoption have only solved one thing: their own infertility. They are not acting for the sake of a child but for the sake of their own need to "play family." Closed adoption parents certainly do not have the child's well-being in mind, since as a result of their own fears and insecurities they only trade one set of problems (a single parent home) for another (genealogical bewilderment).

Those who adopt overseas to make things easier on themselves are also suspect. It's one thing to save an orphaned child from a group home. It's quite another to purchase a baby overseas because you don't want to deal with the child's biologic roots, or because you feel you need a perfect white baby. Going halfway around the world to avoid the birthfamily is cowardly and wrong, but somehow society views these do-gooders in a positive light. There are plenty of adoptable kids right here in the U.S. The question is, is the adoptive family up to the challenge?

8. *Open records for adult adoptees.* Unfortunately [in 1999], we have not yet reached the point where all adoptions are open, so we have an additional problem, that of closed records. How can we say we have the best interests of a child at heart when we tell her she has no right to her original identity? Why are adoptees the only class of people deemed not trustworthy enough to know of their origins? This seems so obvious as to defy further explanation, yet only three states understand it so far. If you believe in basic hu-

man rights, you must grant adoptees the right to know. . . .
The vast majority of birthmothers (some 98%) are for open
records—for they are mothers first, who care about their
children's psychological well-being. Closed records damage
the adoptee, by keeping him forever a child. Adoptees grow
up, but adoption laws do not reflect that obvious fact. They
are never trusted with their heritage. This perpetual infan-
tilization of adoptees is demeaning to all involved, and violates basic constitutional (and property) rights.

9. *Make open adoption agreements legally enforceable.* Only
one state allows birthmothers the protection of open adoption contracts, which help to hold adoptive parents to their
promises. In all other states, such agreements are actually illegal. It's a sad fact that a large percentage of adoptive parents
break their promises for continued contact once they have
the baby in their home. It happens more than you would
think, and is especially tragic when the only reason a birthmother agreed to adoption in the first place was the promise
of ongoing contact with her child. Such agreements must
have the protection given to other serious agreements—the
protection of law.

Birthmothers Don't Ask to Be Created

Birthmothers don't ask to be created. We become, without
wanting to become. We are, without wanting to be. Our mis-
take? Struggling through an unplanned pregnancy in order to
give life, sticking to a strong value system, refusing to care
what others think of our choice. We are told over and over
again during pregnancy, by people who want our oh-so-
valuable babies, that we are doing the honorable thing, making
a beautiful choice, loving our child completely. Then, as soon
as the placement is secure, we are told to be ashamed of what
we have done. We are asked how we could give away blood.
We are shunned and scorned as somehow less than the "real"
adoptive mothers. We hear that "good" birthparents ought to
ride away into the sunset, leaving their children in the past,
leaving the adoptive parents to answer the tough questions and
soothe the child's losses. But fifty years of closed adoption in
the United States has proven that it doesn't work. . . .

Perhaps I seem to be hard on adoptive parents. This is not

because I dislike them, but because they have all the power in adoptive relationships, and therefore far greater responsibilities. The child has no say in what happens to him, and the birthparents lose all rights once the papers are signed. Adoptive parents function as the gods in the adoption triad, and like the gods of mythology they can be either benevolent or terrible. I urge both present and prospective adoptive parents to try to truly feel the enormity of birthmother and adoptee loss. Then, if you still feel the adoption is necessary and good, go ahead with it . . . but do it in a dignified way that honors your child-to-be and the family from which he comes. Then adoption is allowed to be a blessed event, not a disgraceful one.

"Every adopted child also has a birthfather somewhere, but that fact is often ignored."

The Rights of Birth Fathers Must Be Protected

Jeanne Warren Lindsay

In the following viewpoint, Jeanne Warren Lindsay contends that birth fathers are often left out of the adoption process and do not receive adequate counseling or emotional support. She claims that contrary to popular belief, many unmarried young fathers are interested in dealing with unplanned pregnancies and being a part of their children's lives. In addition, failing to honor a birth father's parental rights, she warns, can lead to future legal complications in an adoption. Lindsay founded the Teen Parent Program at Tracy High School in Cerritos, California, and has written various books addressing adolescent pregnancy, parenting, and adoption.

As you read, consider the following questions:
1. According to Lindsay, why did Nick feel his needs as a birth father were not considered?
2. In the author's opinion, for what reasons do birth fathers not participate in adoption planning?
3. According to Lindsay, what happens if the birth father cannot be found?

Excerpted from Jeanne Warren Lindsay, *Pregnant? Adoption Is an Option*. Copyright © 1997 by Jeanne Warren Lindsay. Reprinted by permission of Morning Glory Press, Buena Park, California.

A doption begins with birthparents, yet they are often overlooked in discussions of adoptees and their adoptive families. Even advice columnist Ann Landers tends to put birthparents in the shadows with her tendency to focus on the overriding importance of the adoptive parents.

Even when birthparents are brought out of those shadows, they generally are *birthmothers*. Every adopted child also has a birthfather somewhere, but that fact is often ignored.

Many birthmothers place their babies for adoption because the father won't be parenting his child. The mothers want their children reared in a two-parent family. The birthfather needs to sign the relinquishment papers to make the adoption legal, but other than his signature, he is often out of the picture.

Many birthfathers probably would prefer to be included. Over time in an open adoption, most children would benefit from having the birthfather involved. . . .

Many Birthfathers Do Care

Some men simply don't stick around when they learn their partner is pregnant. That doesn't mean birthfathers as a group don't care. Each birthfather is an individual with unique thoughts and feelings, just as each birthmother is unique. To generalize that birthfathers don't care is a gross injustice to those who do. Sometimes he doesn't appear to care because, for whatever reason, he isn't *allowed* to be involved. . . .

Nick is 25 now, a junior high science teacher and football coach. He was 18 when Kathleen, a year younger, got pregnant. Both he and Kathleen were very active in school. He was co-captain of the football team, she was a musician, and both were college-bound National Honor Society students. . . .

> Kathleen was against abortion, so we assumed we would parent. However, her parents said we couldn't see each other any more, that if they caught us together, Kathleen would be sent off to relatives and I would never see her again. For about two months we communicated only by passing notes at school. Her siblings were there keeping an eye on us. We had to be careful. . . .
>
> Neither of us thought of adoption at first, but her grandmother brought up the idea. She gave us some books and videos to help us learn about it. We talked about it, and we

started going to counseling together. We also went to birth-parent support group and pregnant teen meetings. Through all this, we realized adoption was probably the best solution to our problem.

I think I decided on adoption first because I came from a split home and I knew what it was like to be reared by a single parent. I didn't want to go through a divorce and put my child through what I had experienced. That was a major fear for me. . . .

We talked about it a lot and realized everything wasn't going to be okay. We wanted the best for our daughter, and also what was best for us. Adoption seemed the best plan.

Birthfathers Need Support Too

In spite of Nick's caring concern for Kathleen and their un-born child, and his willingness to attend counseling and support groups with Kathleen, he didn't feel his needs were considered:

The counselor at the agency said something I have never forgotten, something that really bothered me. I was there for Kathleen, I was expected to be there, but the social worker told me there was nothing they could do for me. If I wanted to sit in on Kathleen's counseling sessions, they would allow it, but they didn't have anything going for males. I felt betrayed.

It was a hard time. It was so centered around the female that the male was forgotten. I was very involved and felt connected. I cut the cord, and we took care of our child for three days in the hospital. With all that, I had a lot of emotional ties.

In the past, when birthmothers were expected to give birth, release the baby in a closed adoption, and go home, forgetting the whole experience, many of those birthmoth-ers faced tough times. All birthparents grieve, and we know now that after-placement counseling can be an important part of dealing with that grief. Nick didn't have that help. His life was to go on as if the baby had never happened. He continued his story:

When I went off to college (with a full academic and football scholarship), my life started falling apart. I quit going to class. I lost 30 pounds in one month. I didn't want to get out of bed. I was sick but they couldn't find anything wrong with me. I realize now I was deeply depressed. My relationship with Kathleen had fallen apart, so I had lost my girlfriend and my daughter.

I had a lot of time there at school, several hours a day, that I would just think. I dropped out of school within two months. I didn't get a job, and my family was very upset with me. . . .

As I look back, I realize the support I received around the adoption was not enough. I felt it was my duty to be by Kathleen's side but I wasn't supposed to grieve as she did because I was the male. Males need support too.

Rachel Waldorf, birthmother and, for several years, counselor with Children's Home Society of Minnesota, stressed that counselors' attitudes should be the same toward birthfathers as toward birthmothers. "Sometimes they focus on the birthmother and leave the birthfather out, even if he's sitting right beside her," she commented. "I remember sitting in counseling with my baby's father, and the counselor would look at me and talk to me directly. He was left out.

"There are also attorneys who bad-mouth birthfathers terribly," she added. "You need to find somebody sensitive to birthfathers as well as birthmoms."

If the Birthmother Is Alone

Wendy Heiser, Bethany Christian Services, Seattle, Washington, reports that she works with the birthfather when she can. "I surely encourage it," she said, "but about 98 percent of the time he isn't around. I think he's often scared. He can't afford to parent. It's too bad, because I see it as a time for these men to grow, but a lot of them don't stick around.

"We have our adoptive families write 'Dear Birthfather' along with their 'Dear Birthmother' letters. We encourage him to be supportive for the sake of his child. It's a matter of trying to help them look beyond 'This is my blood' to 'What is best for my child?'". . .

Deane Borgeson of The Adoption Connection, Highland Park, Illinois, reports that about 30 percent of their birthmother clients are involved with the birthfathers. These birthfathers tend to be involved in the adoption process. "Birthmothers really need to understand that for the sake of the baby they should name the birthfather. Otherwise the birthfather can contest an adoption with little effort," Borgeson said.

You may agree that birthfathers *should* be involved, but the birthfather of your baby may even refuse to acknowledge paternity. Or if he doesn't deny he's the father, he may think providing some money will take care of things.

Alexis called the birthfather about her pregnancy. He moved from not believing her to telling her he was sorry and would do anything. Then he called again and said his mother wanted to adopt the baby. Alexis said that wouldn't happen, and from then on he refused to cooperate. Because he would sign no papers, his rights were terminated.

Lisette had broken up with Tom, the birthfather, when she realized she was pregnant. In fact, he was dating a close friend of hers. When he learned about the pregnancy, he offered to provide some money, but said he wanted nothing else to do with the situation. His father was well known in his town and Tom didn't want his parents ever to find out.

Lisette sent him the adoption papers to sign, but he didn't respond. Finally he had to be served the papers, and his parents found out about it. He did sign.

Kernisha felt her baby's father was the loser:

> The father signed the papers but didn't get involved at all. He wasn't there when Scotty was born. Later he asked me if he could have a picture of his son. I gave it to him because I know he missed out on something wonderful. He has a picture, but no memories of Scotty.

Reasons for Non-Involvement

One reason a lot of birthfathers don't get involved in adoption planning, according to Sarah Jensen, director, Adoption Center of San Diego, is their feeling of shame at being unable to parent responsibly at this time. "They think people are saying, 'What kind of man are you?'

"I had one recently who said he was too ashamed to meet the adoptive couple. 'How can a man not take care of his own kid?' he asked. I have had other fathers weep because they know adoption is the right thing for their child, but they feel so powerless. I think birthmothers need to try to understand how the men in their lives are feeling. It's hard for both of them," Jensen concluded.

Sometimes a birthfather is against an adoption plan because he truly wants to parent his child. Other birthfathers may not be interested in active parenting. Instead, he may expect either the birthmother or his own mother to do the parenting.

In either case, a good counselor could help him consider his child's needs as well as his own.

Birthfathers Have Rights

What rights should fathers have in adoption planning? What rights *do* fathers have?

Married couples, of course, normally share parental rights. If a married woman wishes to release her baby for adoption, her husband must also sign the legal relinquishment—even if he is not the child's father.

Years ago, an unmarried father's permission was not required if the mother made an adoption plan. Only the mother's signature was needed. Today, however, the father's signature, if he can be found, is almost always required before the adoption can be finalized.

Putative Father Registries

[Some] states have acted to protect the security of adoption by spelling out what men must do to claim their children.

The clearest trend [in 1998] is the establishment, in 18 states, of "putative father registries" that men must notify if they believe they have impregnated a woman. Typically a man loses his rights unless he registers either before an adoption or soon afterward.

Most experts who have studied this legal approach don't like it. Whatever its intent, they argue, it effectively ensures that birth fathers are excluded from the process, since virtually no one knows the registries exist.

Adam Pertman, *Boston Globe*, March 8, 1998.

If you are considering an adoption plan, and you aren't with your baby's father, it is extremely important that you know the law in your state or province regarding the father's signature in an adoption. Courts and agencies in most states insist that both parents must consent to the release of their child.

If the father can't be found, agencies usually try to locate him. If they can't find him, the court is petitioned to remove the rights of the absent or unknown father. After a certain period of time, the child can then be released for adoption.

Sometimes a birthmother doesn't want her baby's father even to know she's pregnant. Or she may feel he'd be opposed to the adoption plan. She doesn't want him notified. However, a birthfather may be as concerned about his baby's life as is the birthmother. Shutting the father out of the adoption planning can backfire.

If you're in this situation, you need to know the father's legal rights. You don't want the adoption stopped at some later time because he comes back to demand his rights as the child's other parent. You don't want your child's life disrupted after s/he is living with the adoptive family.

If you don't want to talk with him, perhaps you can help your adoption counselor make an appointment with him. When he realizes the ultimate goal of an adoption plan is to provide a good life for his child, and that he may be part of that planning, he may decide to cooperate fully by signing the relinquishment papers. . . .

Both Birthparents Need to Be Involved

Releasing your baby for adoption will be hard. If you decide adoption is the best plan for you and the baby, you want the process to go smoothly for you and your partner, for your baby, and for the adoptive parents.

The father who does not make a decision creates a difficult situation for the mother—and the baby and potential adoptive parents.

If you have decided on or are thinking about releasing your baby for adoption, check the law in your state or province. If you are married, of course both you and your husband must sign the papers. A number of married couples voluntarily release children for adoption each year, according to adoption statistics. If you are single, carefully check with an adoption agency on the laws concerning fathers' rights in your area. It is important to you—and to your baby—that the adoption occur as smoothly as possible.

It is *extremely* important that *all* legal aspects are handled properly. Also important are the birthfather's needs along with the birthmother's. He may want to be involved equally in the planning for his baby's future. While he doesn't have the physical bond of pregnancy, he may form a strong emotional bond with his child.

If your relationship with the birthfather is over, you still need to try to work with him throughout the adoption planning and placement. Getting him involved in planning a placement ceremony for the time you give your baby to the adoptive parents might help him feel included. This is a hard time for him, too.

Making an adoption plan is difficult, whether you are the birthmother or the birthfather. Whichever you are, do all you can to get the help you and your partner will need to make the best possible plan for your baby, and then to handle the loss of your child to the adoptive family.

It won't be easy for either of you.

> *"Courts have recognized a duty to disclose known material information about a child's health and social background to prospective adoptive families."*

The Rights of Adoptive Parents Must Be Protected

Madelyn Freundlich and Lisa Peterson

In wrongful adoption, a child placement agency fails to disclose or misrepresents vital health or background information of a child to the adoptive family. In the following viewpoint, Madelyn Freundlich and Lisa Peterson contend that wrongful adoptions highlight the need for greater protection of the rights of adoptive parents. The authors make several recommendations designed to safeguard adoptive families and children from wrongful adoption. Freundlich is executive director of the Evan B. Donaldson Adoption Institute, an organization dedicated to improving adoption practices and policies, and author of numerous books on adoption. Peterson is legal consultant to Spence-Chaplin Services to Families and Children, a nonprofit child placement agency.

As you read, consider the following questions:
1. In Freundlich and Peterson's opinion, how can disclosure of medical or background information benefit adoptees?
2. According to the authors, why do agency staff not obtain information from birth parents?
3. What recommendations do Freundlich and Peterson suggest to adoption agencies to make sure that adoptive parents know the risks of an adoption?

From Madelyn Freundlich and Lisa Peterson, *Wrongful Adoption: Law, Policy, and Practice*; © 1998. Reprinted by special permission of the Child Welfare League of America, Washington, D.C.

Adoption agencies increasingly have confronted issues about obtaining and disclosing information to prospective adoptive families about the health and social background of children and their birth families. Quality practice supports the sharing of such information. Litigation related to this issue has shown, however, that in a number of cases, adoption agencies and independent practitioners have failed to provide prospective adoptive families with known information about a child's physical, emotional, or developmental problems or with critical background information about the child's birth family and history. In these cases, adoptive families, deprived of such information, have found themselves neither emotionally nor financially prepared to care for a child whose needs require enormously expensive medical or mental health treatment. Some of these families have sought redress in the courts.

In response to litigation initiated by adoptive families, courts have recognized a duty to disclose known material information about a child's health and social background to prospective adoptive families. Although the duty to disclose applies to agencies and independent practitioners alike, most of the cases to date have involved agencies. In the face of a breach of the duty to disclose, courts have held agencies liable for the tort of "wrongful adoption" and awarded adoptive families monetary damages. An agency's breach of the duty to disclose can take many forms and, depending on the state, liability may be imposed when agencies misrepresent a child's background, deliberately withhold information, or are negligent in providing prospective adoptive parents with information that could be material to their decision whether to adopt a particular child. . . .

The Benefits of Disclosure

The importance of disclosing health and other background information is now well recognized by adoption professionals. The benefits of full disclosure flow to children who are placed for adoption, their birth families, prospective adoptive parents, and the adoptive family. For children, disclosure of complete and accurate background information may

- enhance opportunities for early diagnosis and treatment

of physical, medical, and psychological problems and conditions;
- promote earlier identification of developmental delays and mobilization of early intervention services to maximize the child's development;
- avoid the need for unnecessary or duplicative testing;
- assist in preventing and/or reducing the risks associated with certain physical or emotional problems;
- provide information that would be important to the adopted adult's own childbearing decisions and information related to the health of his or her descendants; and
- provide critical information to assist the adopted individual, both in childhood and adulthood, in developing a sense of history about himself or herself and a more fully integrated identity.

For birth parents, the agency's collection of health and other background information and disclosure of that information to the child's adoptive parents provide important reassurances. These practices communicate the commitment of the agency to assisting the adoptive family in understanding and meeting the child's needs and to assuring that the child will have important information about his or her origins.

For prospective adoptive parents, disclosure of complete and accurate health and other background information about a child facilitates informed decision making. Advising adoptive families of known health and other background information is a critical step toward assuring that families are emotionally and financially prepared to meet a child's special needs. Disclosing such information provides the family with opportunities to seek and obtain adoption subsidies and other resources that the child may need. When families make the decision to adopt based on complete and accurate information, they are far more likely to be prepared to meet the child's current and future needs and to assist the child with identity issues as the child grows and develops. Informed decision making and planning by adoptive families is likely to reduce the possibility of adoption disruption and its consequent trauma on children.

Despite the recognized benefits of full and accurate disclosure, recent legal developments illustrate that agencies and independent practitioners have not uniformly disclosed to prospective adoptive parents known health and other background information on children. . . .

A number of reasons have been advanced to explain agencies' failures to disclose. Listed below are explanations that are frequently given for these failures:

Fear that children will not be placed if their histories are known leads to hesitancy to disclose information. . . .

Social workers may believe that prospective adoptive families are interested only in healthy children; they may not recognize the benefits for children and adoptive families when background information is fully and accurately shared; or they may fear that if prospective adoptive families were given all the relevant health and other background information, they would decline to adopt the children who need adoptive families. . . .

Agency staff do not obtain the needed information from birth parents. . . .

Practitioners agree that staff may not always obtain all needed information from birth parents. These problems may involve good faith failures to ask certain questions; lack of diligence in asking and following up on questions that could lead to relevant information; and other difficulties, including limited skills in assisting birth families in disclosing sensitive information that they may be reluctant or unwilling to share.

Agency staff lack access to complete medical histories from sending countries.

In the context of international adoptions, agencies' failure to disclose health and other background information is often attributed to their inability to obtain full and accurate information from the sending countries. This may be the case notwithstanding an agency's diligent and repeated requests for such information. In addition, the limited information that is received often is not reliable because of the nature of pediatric services available abroad, which often are more limited than in the United States in terms of screening, diagnostic evaluation, and treatment.

Breakdowns in communication result from understaffing and worker turnover.

In addition to problems associated with obtaining full and accurate information, some writers have pointed to problems in completely and accurately communicating that information. Some agencies agree with this assessment, pointing to oversized caseloads that limit the time that staff have to devote to each adoptive placement and frequent changes in staff which make it difficult to ensure that the necessary information is communicated. . . .

Recommendations for Practice

The law on wrongful adoption provides guidance on the duty of agencies and independent practitioners to disclose health and other background information to prospective adoptive parents. The cases and state disclosure statutes make clear that liability will be imposed if agencies fail to disclose known material health and other background information about a child and the child's birth family. Agencies may not misrepresent the child's background, portraying it as more favorable than the agency knows it to be, nor may agencies deliberately conceal unfavorable information. Agencies are also required, at a minimum, to communicate known information if asked by prospective adoptive parents and, when volunteering information, to impart known information fully and accurately. Expanding on that requirement, some courts recently have imposed a duty on agencies to provide all material health and other background information in the agency's possession, irrespective of whether the prospective adoptive parents specifically ask for that information or whether the agency prefers to remain silent. . . .

There are a number of steps that agencies may take to ensure quality practice in disclosing health and other background information and, thereby limit their exposure to liability for wrongful adoption. . . . Attention to issues related to insurance coverage for potential wrongful adoption liability is also critical to an agency's planning and practice in this area.

Agencies can improve practice and limit exposure to wrongful adoption liability by taking steps in the following areas:

- Obtaining and disclosing material health and other background information;

- Educating prospective adoptive parents about the limits on information gathering and disclosure;
- Heightening adoptive parents' awareness about their own responsibilities in reaching an informed decision about whether to adopt a particular child;
- Providing adoptive parents with written disclosure of health and other background information and with documents that describe the risks and uncertainties associated with adoption, and
- Staff training.

Material Health and Other Background Information

Agencies should use the concept of "materiality" to guide the collection and disclosure of health and other background information. Material information is any information that may be important to a prospective adoptive parent in deciding whether to adopt a particular child. It is the failure to disclose this type of information that deprives prospective adoptive parents of an opportunity to make an informed decision and that places agencies at risk of liability for wrongful adoption. Agencies should have processes in place to ensure that material information is obtained from birth families and is communicated to prospective adoptive parents.

Collection of material health and other background information involves work with birth parents to elicit, through counseling and sensitive questioning, medical history, family background, and other information bearing on the child's health and developmental status. In addition to interviews with birth parents, there are specific strategies that agencies can use to enhance the quality and reliability of the health and other background information they obtain. Specifically with regard to collection of health information, agencies may use birth parent medical questionnaires, obtain and review hospital and other health care records, and ensure that children have physical examinations immediately prior to placement. Agencies should also develop clear policies and guidelines on collection and disclosure of social and family background information and disclosure of information on children's HIV status. . . .

Educating Prospective Adoptive Parents

Prospective adoptive parents should be helped to understand how health and other background information is obtained. In the case of domestic infant adoptions, they should be told that usually the sole source of information concerning children is the birth parents and, in many cases, only the birth mother. Birth parents may be reluctant to share certain information about family medical or mental health history. In other instances, the information they have may be limited if only because their own parents (the adoptee's biological grandparents) are relatively young and not yet affected by many of the conditions associated with middle age. In international adoptions, the prospective adoptive parents should be helped to understand that the sole source of information is the agency in the sending country, which may have limited access to health and social information about a child. . . .

Agencies should clearly communicate to prospective adoptive parents that there are risks inherent in adoption, just as there are risks in any form of parenting. Prospective

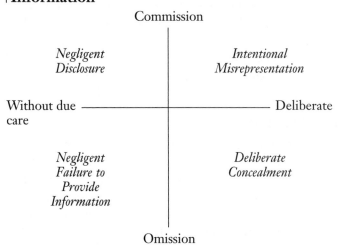

Bases for Liability: Failure to Disclose Material Health and Other Background Information

Commission

Negligent Disclosure

Intentional Misrepresentation

Without due care ——————————————— Deliberate

Negligent Failure to Provide Information

Deliberate Concealment

Omission

Madelyn Freundlich and Lisa Peterson, *Wrongful Adoption: Law, Policy, and Practice*, 1998.

adoptive parents should be helped to understand that, by pursuing adoption, they will be assuming responsibilities for which there are no guarantees of specific results or outcomes. Key to practice in this area is communicating to prospective adoptive parents that notwithstanding an agency's best efforts to obtain and disclose health and other background information, it is not possible to provide an assurance that all existing information has been discovered nor is it possible to predict the future health status of a child. . . .

Agencies should provide adoptive parents with written information on the health and social background of the child and ensure that adoptive parents sign, acknowledging receipt of the information. Whenever possible, agencies should provide copies of reports, assessments, or other documentation contained in other records, rather than summarizing material. Summaries tend to include interpretations of the meaning or significance of the information and increase the likelihood of errors in transcription. When materials are provided to prospective adoptive parents on multiple pages, the adoptive parents should initial each page, indicating that they have reviewed the entire document.

In addition to disclosing health and other background information itself, it is important that agencies clearly communicate to prospective adoptive parents certain cautions related to proceeding to adopt on the basis of known health and other background information. Providing these caveats in writing reiterates for adoptive parents the risks and uncertainties involved in adoption and, at the same time, helps to protect agencies from claims of wrongful adoption. . . .

Staff Training

A final area on which agencies should focus is staff training. Agencies should ensure that staff are thoroughly familiar with standards of quality practice in collecting and communicating health and other background information. Staff should have a clear understanding of the importance of such information for the child, the birth family, prospective adoptive parents, and the adoptive family. Staff also should have skills in working with birth families to obtain needed information and in fully and accurately conveying that information to prospective adoptive families. Staff should be familiar with and able to effectively use the agency's required documentation related to the gathering and disclosure of health and other background information.

Equally important in staff development is attention to the attitudes that staff may have about adoption in relation to gathering and sharing background information. A staff member's own perspectives, experiences, and biases may impact his or her own work in this area, and self-awareness and acknowledgment of personal views can greatly enhance practice. For example, at one agency, a staff member conducting initial information sessions for persons interested in international adoption regularly begins by encouraging prospective adoptive parents to recognize that adoption (like life itself) is full of risks. She openly identifies herself as being, personally, a risktaker and tells parents that international adoption has risks that she would readily take but that are not appropriate for everyone, including the potential that a child will experience developmental delays as a result of early institutionalization. Similarly, a social worker at another agency who speaks with prospective adoptive parents about children with Down's Syndrome regularly discloses that her own brother is affected by Down's Syndrome. Through sharing that information, she gives families an opportunity to talk to someone with personal experience and conveys to them that her own experience and outlook may be different from their own. Agencies can help staff develop the knowledge and skills they need in the area of information collection and disclosure by providing opportunities for staff to identify their personal views and experiences and integrate those aspects into their professional practice.

"First and foremost, the adoption professional should regard adoption as a service to children who need permanent families."

The Rights of the Child Must Be Protected

L. Anne Babb

L. Anne Babb is executive director of the Family Tree Adoption Counseling Center in Norman, Oklahoma, a nonprofit adoption advocacy organization, and coauthor of *Adopting and Advocating for the Special Needs Child*. In the following viewpoint, Babb claims that in order to achieve ethical standards in adoption, the rights of the child should be paramount. She contends that the main purpose of adoption is to serve the needs of the child. To fulfill their needs, children in adoption must have the right to be raised in their families of origin when possible, be permitted to maintain kinship ties, and have access to information about themselves.

As you read, consider the following questions:
1. In the author's opinion, how can adoption professionals discourage "black market" adoptions?
2. According to Babb, how can adoption professionals respect adoptees?
3. In Babb's view, what information must be shared to ensure that an adoptee's history is fully disclosed?

First and foremost, the adoption professional should regard adoption as a service to children who need permanent families.

Nondiscrimination should be observed in counseling adoptees and in the adoptive placement of children needing the service. The adoption professional should neither practice nor condone discrimination on the basis of race, gender, sexual orientation, age, religion, national origin, mental or physical handicap, or any other preferential or personal characteristic of children entering into the adoption process, except insofar as such qualities can be *demonstrated* to have a negative impact on a particular proposed or actual adoptive placement and with regard to a specific child. The adoption professional should not allow any such characteristic to unreasonably postpone or prevent the permanent adoptive placement of a child needing the service of adoption.

Protecting the Child's Rights

Protect the child's right to grow up in his or her family of origin. The adoption professional should, to the best of his or her ability, see to it that children can be cared for by their own parents, or, in the case of failing parental care, by a member of the extended family.

Protect the child's right to grow up with his or her siblings. The adoption professional should value the sibling relationship of children living in foster and adoptive families and, to the best of his or her ability, see to it that children are placed with their siblings. When placement with siblings is not in the best interests of a child, the professional should foster ongoing contact between siblings whenever possible. Information about the existence and whereabouts of siblings and half-siblings should be a permanent part of the information that travels with the child.

Protect the child's right to grow up in his or her own community. The adoption professional should safeguard the child's right to grow up in his or her own community, culture, race, nation, and religion and should support intercountry adoption only when adoption within the child's own community is unavailable.

Oppose black and gray market adoptions. The adoption professional should not participate in adoptions in which illegal, illicit, or unethical behavior occurs among adoption facilitators, whether those facilitators are professionals or not. The professional should not condone the behavior or policies of others, including agencies and attorneys, that treat adoption service as an industry and adoptees as commodities.

Supporting the Child

Provide age-appropriate adoption counseling. The adoption professional should explain the adoption process to the child needing the service in an age-appropriate way through the use of words, pictures, videotapes, the Life Book, play, and any other means available to him or her.

Allow for the child's consent and participation in adoption when possible. When a child cannot remain with his or her birth parents, the adoption professional should consider the child's wishes and opinions and encourage him or her to participate in the adoption process and give consent to being adopted verbally and in writing, as appropriate to the child's age, circumstances, emotional health, cognitive abilities, and development.

Facilitate grieving. When a child older than infancy leaves his or her birth family, the adoption professional should give the child the opportunity to say good-bye to his or her parents, siblings, pets, neighbors and friends, and other loved ones and should help the child through counseling for grief, separation, and loss. The adoption professional should be prepared to address the adoptee's developmental needs to re-cycle through the grief process throughout the lifespan.

Give adoptees information about themselves. The adoption professional recognizes and supports the right of the minor adoptee, with the permission of the adoptive parents, and the adult adoptee to have information about him or herself, including his or her name at birth; social, medical, psychological, educational, cultural, and racial background; birth parents' history; and reason for relinquishment.

The adoption professional understands the adoptee's need for a personal history and supports the need by safeguarding informational narratives, videotapes, photographs, heirlooms, gifts, and clothing given to the child by his or her parents and caretakers, entrusting such items to those who will be equally respectful of the importance of such objects.

Give adoptees information about their culture. In all cases of transracial, transcultural, or intercountry adoption, the adoption professional gives adoptees the opportunity to have information about their culture of origin. The adoption professional works with agencies and organizations to give the adoptee cultural and ethnic activities such as camps, homeland tours, and buddy families of the adoptee's cultural or ethnic background, along with written information and bibliographies that emphasize the child's ethnic group, culture, and original nationality.

Give adoptees information about their rights. The adoption professional should advise adult adoptees of their rights, where legally applicable, to have copies of all legal documents related to their births, including their original birth certificates and adoption (amended birth) certificates and adoption decrees. Where such legal rights do not exist, the adoption professional should advocate for such rights on behalf of adult adoptees.

Adoptee-adoptive parent matching. The adoption professional should choose adoptive parents who will best be able to meet the needs of the adopted child.

Continue to serve the client. The adoption professional should not abandon or neglect the adoptee after an adoption has been finalized. Postplacement services to adoptees should be available, the adoptee and his or her parents advised that they are available, and they should be provided as needed.

Respecting the Child

Respect the adoptee. The adoption professional should divest him- or herself of adoption mythology and refuse to define the adoptee's reality for him or her by describing the adoptee as "chosen, lucky" or in negative terms, such as "ungrateful," or by using words like "illegitimate, bastard.". . .

Support the kinship system. The extended families of the mother and father should be considered first when adoption is chosen as a plan for a child. The parents, siblings, aunts, uncles, and cousins of the birth parents should be considered as possible guardians or adoptive parents of the child if adoption is chosen, before strangers are asked to assume such responsibilities. If relative placement is not an option, the adoption professional should make every effort to preserve connections of some kind between children going into adoption and their birth families.

Reprinted by permission of Mike Luckovich and Creators Syndicate, Inc.

Explain and offer open adoption. Professionals who arrange open adoptions should provide older waiting children with complete and accurate information about open adoption and guardianship, including the legal enforceability or unenforceability of such arrangements and the enforceability or unenforceability of continued contact with the children's birth and former foster families. Older children should be given information about the effect of adoption on their ongoing contact with siblings and relatives.

Be respectful of the waiting child during adoptive family recruitment. The adoption professional regards the child in need of permanency through adoption as of equal value to other children and uses respect, care, and caution through efforts to recruit an adoptive family for a child or sibling group. Children should not be advertised or families recruited for them in such a way that a child might be subjected to ridicule or judgment by his or her peers or otherwise harmed through such recruitment efforts.

When considering the use of photolisting, videotape recruitment, and "matching parties," the professional should approach all efforts by asking how the professional would want his or her own child to be presented to the world. When a child is old enough to consent to recruitment efforts, he or she should participate in the decision making and have the opportunity to review materials advertising his or her availability for adoption.

Avoid undue influence. The adoption professional understands the adoptee's search for his or her birth relatives as a normative aspect of having been adopted. The adoption professional avoids putting any responsibility on the adoptee for the feelings of the adoptive parents. Instead, the adoption professional provides printed resources and referrals to other professionals or groups who can help the adoptive parents cope with the adoptee's search, possible reunion, and possible ongoing contact with the birth family. . . .

Providing Services for the Child

Adoptees should be referred to available local, regional, and national groups that can give them support for issues specific to their individual circumstances (e.g., groups for adolescent adoptees, internationally adopted persons, transracially adopted persons, adoptees searching for birth parents, etc.).

Fully disclose adoptee history. Adoption professionals, workers, and agencies should disclose all known background information concerning the prospective adoptee to the adoptive parents prior to placement. The history should include social, psychological, medical, educational, and emotional histories as well as information about and access to all former caretakers and the birth family of the child. This same information should be available to the adult adoptee or to the minor adoptee with the agreement of the adoptive parent(s).

Provide information about specialized treatment. Some children who are older at the time of adoption and who have emotional or psychiatric problems will need residential treat-

ment or other specialized mental health help. Prior to placement, the adoption professional should teach adoptive parents about such needs and about resources for treatment in
the community, state, and surrounding regions. The adoption professional should tell adoptive parents about what financial assistance, if any, is available for such treatment, how
much it will be, and its duration. The adoption professional
should also inform adoptive parents about costs not covered
by assistance programs, if any, and what the cost of such
treatment would be in the event that adoption assistance
payments, Medicaid, and other federal or state programs are
reduced or eliminated.

The adoption professional should inform birth parents
and adoptees about specialized services available in the community that will assist them with issues surrounding adoption, grief, loss, identity formation, and other adoption-
related concerns.

Periodical Bibliography

The following articles have been selected to supplement the diverse views presented in this chapter. Addresses are provided for periodicals not indexed in the *Readers' Guide to Periodical Literature*, the *Alternative Press Index*, the *Social Sciences Index*, or the *Index to Legal Periodicals and Books*.

Pam Belluck	"In Tug-of-War Over a Toddler, a Cry of Politics," *New York Times*, September 19, 1999.
Daniel Evans	"Judge Criticizes County for Not Notifying Mom of Kids' Adoption," *Los Angeles Daily Journal*, October 13, 2000. Available from Los Angeles Daily Journal, 915 E. First St., Los Angeles, CA 90012.
William Glaberson	"Case Tries to Win Siblings' Right to Be Together," *New York Times*, December 29, 1998.
Liane Leshre	"Wrongful Adoption, Fewer Secrets and Lies, But Agencies Fail at Full Disclosure," *Trial*, April 1999.
Mary Otto	"Mothers Who 'Discard' Babies Often Scared, Confused, Alone," *San Diego Union-Tribune*, March 26, 1999.
Catherine Sakach	"Withdrawal of Consent for Adoption: Allocating the Risk," *Whittier Law Review*, Fall 1997.
Gary Spencer	"Panel Revives Claim of Wrongful Adoption, Family Alleges Child's Past Was Concealed," *New York Law Journal*, May 10, 1999. Available online from www.law.com/ny.
Barbara White Stack	"Parental Rights," *IRE Journal*, May/June 2000. Available from Investigative Reporters and Editors, Inc., 138 Neff Annex, Missouri School of Journalism, Columbia, MO 65211.
Wall Street Journal	"Suffer the Children," *Wall Street Journal*, October 15, 1999.
Daniel Wise	"Teen Father's Rights Restored in Adoption," *New York Law Journal*, November 22, 1999. Available online from www.law.com/ny.

CHAPTER 3

What Types of Adoption Should Be Encouraged?

Chapter Preface

Some children are especially difficult to place with adoptive families because they have "special needs." Many of these children have physical, mental, or emotional disabilities. Others wait longer in foster care because they are older, belong to a group of siblings who should be kept together, or come from minority ethnic backgrounds. The challenge of finding adoptive parents able to care for special needs children may delay their chances for adoption.

Conventional policies are geared to facilitate adoptions by married couples and same-race placements. Many adoption advocates contend that this approach shrinks the pool of potential parents for special needs children. As a result, they have promoted adoptions undertaken by nontraditional families, which include transracial adoptions and adoptions by gay, lesbians, and single parents. For instance, the U.S. Department of Health and Human Resources reports that in 2000, 33 percent of children in foster care were adopted by a single parent. In addition, single adults tend to file more special needs adoptions than married couples.

Although single parent adoptions are the least controversial among nontraditional forms of parenting, such adoptive placements are criticized. Opponents argue that single parenting is inferior to that provided by married couples. According to family research professional Richard B. Knight, children of single parents are at higher risk of early sexual activity, drug abuse, and delinquency. Other detractors contend that children need both male and female parenting in order to develop healthy identities. According to one study, boys raised in female-headed households developed more identity issues than boys brought up by heterosexual couples.

Advocates of single parent adoption claim that children raised by single adoptive parents do just as well as their counterparts. In one follow-up study, single parents and couples similarly rated the development of their adopted children's physical and emotional health. Other supporters insist that single adults are characteristically enabled to face the challenges of parenthood. Adoption expert E. Branham reports that single parent adoption applicants, in general, are emotionally mature, can cope with high levels of stress, and have supportive familial connections.

Whether or not nontraditional adoptions suit children's needs is discussed in the following chapter, "What Types of Adoption Should Be Encouraged?"

"The voices of African-American adult transracial adoptees show . . . a positive public image and opinion about the concept of transracial adoptive placements."

Transracial Adoptions Should Be Encouraged

Kirsten Wonder Albrecht

Kirsten Wonder Albrecht is the president of the TransRacial Adoption Group (TRA Group), an international organization that is dedicated to finding permanent adoptive homes for minority children and coordinating support groups for transracial adoptees and their families. In the following viewpoint, Albrecht contends that transracial adoptions should be encouraged because efforts to find minority homes for minority children are often unsuccessful and result in the child's placement in foster or institutional care settings. She argues that existing transracial adoption practices discourage potential parents from adopting minority children, prolonging the period that such children endure living in harmful or unstable environments.

As you read, consider the following questions:

1. According to the author, what are some ways transracial adoption practices discourage prospective adoptive parents?
2. How does Albrecht support her argument that the cultural competence tests are unfair to whites?
3. What evidence does Albrecht cite to support her claim that African American transracial adoptees generally support transracial adoptions?

Reprinted from Kirsten Wonder Albrecht's testimony before the U.S. House of Representatives Ways and Means Committee, Subcommittee on Human Resources, September 15, 1998.

The TransRacial Adoption Group is committed to promoting transracial adoptive placements as a viable form of adoption. Its mission is to find permanent homes for the hundreds of thousands of minority children languishing in various child welfare systems. The agenda is to dispel the myth that same-race placements are always preferable to transracial placements and to challenge current adoption agency practices that continue to create obstacles for white parents and interracial couples interested in adopting black and biracial children in the United States.

Despite the enactment of the InterEthnic Adoption Amendment [passed in 1996 to remove barriers to interracial adoption], white prospective adoptive parents and interracial couples continue to face hurdles in their attempts to adopt black and biracial children. My objective for the prepared testimony is to support this statement by presenting 3 major points:

- Although the National Association of Black Social Workers (NABSW) has publicly retreated from its adamant opposition to transracial adoptions, black social workers continue to impede transracial adoptive placements. The most notable new obstacle is the cultural competence test.
- A majority of white couples and single parents who have completed an international transracial adoption report that they first tried but were unsuccessful in completing a domestic transracial adoption.
- A majority of adult transracial adoptees have very favorable opinions of transracial adoptions and strongly disagree with the National Association of Black Social Workers' position that black and biracial children cannot develop a positive sense of racial identity in white adoptive homes.

Current Obstacles

In the *National Transracial Adoptive Families Population Survey: Initial Report on Prospective Adoptive Parents*, the TRA Group documents the major obstacles prospective adoptive white parents and interracial couples currently experience in each of the six major phases of the process to adopt a black or biracial child in the United States. In the information gathering phase, prospective adoptive parents are constantly discouraged from considering adopting a black or biracial child. The intake service caseworkers bombard the prospective adoptive parents with the alleged difficulties involved in transracial adoptive placements and question the motives of the prospective adoptive parents. In the application phase, as compared to prospective adoptive black parents, prospective adoptive white parents experience greater delays in the processing of their paperwork. It is not uncommon for home evaluations to be constantly postponed, for important application files or background checks to mysteriously disappear or for unfair allegations to be made against white families by black social workers.

In the licensing phase, prospective adoptive parents are often required to attend foster parent training classes which once again bombard the prospective adoptive parents with the alleged horror stories of transracial adoptive placements. Unfortunately, some states' training classes are actually taught by members of the National Association of Black Social Workers which publicly opposes transracial adoptive placements. In the child selection phase, prospective adoptive parents are often told that particular children they are interested in adopting are not available. Caseworkers and state adoption departments are slow to initiate parental termination hearings so that the children are not yet legally available for adoption. These same caseworkers are quick to articulate that particular children are "already being adopted by a black family," when in many instances a prospective black family does not exist, or in other cases, the prospective black family's income is below federal standards for poverty.

In the foster-care placement phase, white foster parents caring for a black or biracial child are constantly told not to get attached to the child because the placement is only temporary. Caseworkers inform prospective adoptive white foster families that the agency is looking for a black adoptive home or planning to reunite the child with his/her birth parent. When the child has remained in the home for several years, many white foster families often express an interest in adopting the child. However, their interest is met with opposition—some foster-care licenses are mysteriously revoked or the children are suddenly removed from the home thereby eliminating the foster parents' right to be included in any future legal hearings concerning the child. Finally, in the adoption phase, prospective adoptive white parents often encounter objections to the transracial adoption at the petition for adoption hearing. It is not uncommon for black birth mothers to suddenly resurface and claim they gave no consent to the adoption, or for long lost African-American relatives to suddenly express an interest in adopting the child, or for expert witnesses to testify to persuade the judge that transracial adoptions are not in the "best interest of the child."

The Cultural Competence Test

The newest weapon added to the arsenal to eliminate transracial adoptive placements is the development of a cultural competence test. Social workers opposed to transracial adoptions are now arguing that white parents need to pass a "black test" in order to qualify to adopt and raise a minority child. In academic circles, cultural competency is defined as the ability to work effectively with members from different cultural, religious or ethnic groups. However, in the adoption arena, it is a test to determine if white parents "are black enough" to develop a positive cultural identity in their adopted children.

Some tests might award points to prospective parents who live in an integrated neighborhood, attend an interracial religious organization, or subscribe to *Ebony* magazine. Other tests might deduct points for prospective parents who have no African-American friends or are not interested in celebrating Kwanza or were raised in the South. Some social workers might envision a test that was actually presented at a deposition to a white foster mother in Ohio who was attempting to adopt two black foster children. A lawyer representing a black couple interested in adopting the same children asked the white foster mother to identify the following list of names—James Weldon Johnson, Dr. Mae C. Jemison, P.B.S. Pinchback, Shirley Chisolm, Dr. Ralph J. Bunche, and Ethel Waters. The attorney was attempting to show that if the white foster mother failed to recognize these names she was an unfit mother.

The problem with the cultural competence concept is two-fold. First, it fails to reflect the true diversity within the African-American community by assuming that all African-Americans do that which is to be required of white adoptive parents. Why should white adoptive families have to celebrate Kwanza when it is not celebrated in a majority of African-American homes? Which African-American community should be the model—the inner city, the rural south, or the suburban professional?

Range of Advantages

There is no evidence that black parents do a better job than white parents of raising black children with a sense of pride in their racial heritage and culture. . . . Critics of transracial adoption have claimed that only blacks can teach black children the coping skills needed for life in a racist society, but there seems at least as good an argument for the proposition that whites are in the best position to teach black children how to maneuver in the white worlds of power and privilege. Indeed it seems clear that for black children growing up in a white-dominated world, there would be a range of material advantages associated with having white parents and living in the largely white and relatively privileged world that such parents tend to frequent.

Elizabeth Bartholet, *University of Pennsylvania Law Review*, 1991.

Second, a cultural competence concept would effectively eliminate the purpose of the InterEthnic Adoption Amendment. Prior to the MultiEthnic Placement Act (MEPA) and the amendment, it was not uncommon for a social worker to write in a report denying a transracial adoptive placement "denied because white." This is now considered a blatant violation of the statutes. The cultural competence test would allow a social worker to deny a transracial adoptive placement by writing "white parent failed to braid black child's hair." This would effectively allow the discrimination to continue but in a more subtle form.

More importantly, individuals advocating for the cultural competence test ought to consider that a majority of African-American prospective adoptive parents could not correctly identify the individuals listed above as the composer of *Lift Every Voice and Sing*, the first African-American woman in space, the first African-American governor, the first African-American congresswoman, the first African-American Nobel Peace Prize recipient, and an actress/singer.

A Difficult Journey

It is a difficult journey for prospective adoptive white parents and interracial couples interested in adopting a black or bi-racial child from a public adoption agency. It is not surprising that many prospective adoptive parents decide that it is easier to pursue an international or private adoption; thus denying a black or biracial child currently in our beleaguered foster care system an opportunity for a permanent home. In the *National Transracial Adoptive Families Population Survey: Initial Report on International Transracial Adoptive Parents*, the TRA Group received disappointing confirmation that the domestic trans-racial adoption process can be so overwhelming that some parents opt out of the system entirely. Out of the approximate 12,000 families who completed an international transracial adoption in 1997, 87 percent of the 1,000 families surveyed reported that the international transracial adoption was completed only after unsuccessfully attempting to adopt a black or biracial child from the United States. It is disheartening to learn that available homes were denied to minority children in foster care.

For many foster parents caring for a black or biracial child, an attempt to adopt the child is often met with great opposition. In the *National Transracial Adoptive Families Population Survey: Initial Report on Transracial Foster Parents*, the TRA Group received alarming reports from families that were forced to resort to litigation in order to adopt their foster children. In 1997 alone, 12 lawsuits in 11 states were filed alleging civil rights violations for racially discriminatory adoption practices. As of September 1998, 4 of the lawsuits have settled. Twenty-two other families reported filing complaints with the Office of Civil Rights. Forty-five other families have contacted the TRA Group to report intentions to file civil rights lawsuits. In all, the TRA Group received reports from 500 families describing conduct that appears to blatantly violate the InterEthnic Adoption Amendment.

New Perspectives on Transracial Adoption

Against this backdrop, it is important to highlight the results of the first in-depth examination of adult transracial adoptees' public perceptions about the debate and controversy surrounding transracial adoptive placements. In the *National Transracial Adoptive Families Population Survey: Initial Report on Perceptions of Adult Transracial Adoptees*, the TRA Group conducted a survey based on telephone interviews with a random representative sample of 405 African-American transracial adoptees over the age of 18 living in the United States. The sample data were weighted to bring the sample characteristics into alignment with the demographics of the 10,000 adult transracial adoptees in the TRA Group's registry database.

Most transracial adoptees had a favorable opinion of transracial adoptions. Virtually all adoptees strongly disagreed with the National Association of Black Social Workers view of transracial adoption as a form of "cultural genocide." Instead, adoptees expressed opinions that white homes should be viewed as viable adoptive homes, not just as a second best alternative, for black and biracial children currently languishing in foster care.

- 97 percent of the participants agreed with the statement that white adoptive parents are capable of developing a positive sense of cultural identity in an adopted black child.
- 86 percent of the participants did not believe that a preference should always be given to an African-American couple when both the black family and white family are interested in adopting the same black child.
- 93 percent of the participants did not think it was necessary for an adoption agency to first search for a qualified black family when a white foster family was interested in adopting their black foster child.

Although some African-American groups have traditionally opposed transracial adoptive placements, the voices of African-American adult transracial adoptees show a "new perspective"—one that reflects a positive public image and opinion about the concept of transracial adoptive placements and their own experiences.

Removing Racial Prejudice

Some believe that the InterEthnic Adoption Amendment is just like any other radically new legislation. It took time to implement the Civil Rights Act; it will take time to implement the InterEthnic Adoption Amendment. Unfortunately, the 500,000 minority children languishing in foster care do not have time at their disposal. Agencies must be held accountable for their racially discriminatory adoption practices. Most of the burden currently falls on individual families motivated to make change through lawsuits. Some of the burden must be shifted to the Office of Civil Rights (OCR). OCR must continue to actively investigate reports and issue compliance requirements to adoption agencies.

Changing the written law is one thing. Changing the personal prejudices of a group of people required to implement the law is another thing. The InterEthnic Adoption Amendment is a very important piece of legislation but it is only the beginning in a long journey to remove racial prejudice from the child welfare system.

2

"*[Solving] the overrepresentation of children of color in the child welfare system by protecting transracial adoption . . . fails to protect those who are most vulnerable in this society.*"

Same-Race Adoptions Should Be Encouraged

Leslie Doty Hollingsworth

Many adoption advocates are in favor of increasing transracial adoptions to respond to the overrepresentation of minority children in the child welfare system. However, adoption expert Leslie Doty Hollingsworth contends that the promotion of same-race adoptions is a more desirable solution to the disproportionate numbers of minority children in foster care. In the following viewpoint, Hollingsworth argues that to meet the needs of adoptable minority children, policies and attitudes must be changed to encourage more minority families to adopt. In addition, she claims public policies should support family preservation and counter the forces that negatively impact minority families, such as social inequality and poverty. Hollingsworth is assistant professor at the School of Social Work at the University of Michigan.

As you read, consider the following questions:
1. According to Hollingsworth, what claims are used to promote transracial adoption?
2. In Hollingsworth's opinion, what organizational barriers prevent minority parents from adopting?
3. What are some recommendations the author makes to lessen the need for transracial adoption?

Reprinted, with permission, from "Promoting Same-Race Adoption for Children of Color," by Leslie Doty Hollingsworth, *Social Work*, vol. 43, no. 2, (1998), pp. 104–16. Copyright © 1998, National Association of Social Workers, Inc.

The adoption of orphaned children from other countries by U.S. families began in the 1940s with the end of World War II. A rise in the number of such adoptions accompanied later wars, including the Korean and Vietnam Wars. In the 1960s, widespread use of artificial birth control, the legalization of abortion, and decreased social stigma associated with bearing a child outside of marriage were accompanied by a substantial decrease in healthy white infants available for adoption. There was, however, no corresponding decrease among African American and other children of color (although foreign countries began to establish rules that limited some adoptions in those countries).

Feeling the Pressure

It has been suggested that adoption agencies, feeling the pressure of reduced fee income, found in the availability of children of color an opportunity to increase adoption fees. One writer suggested that as the United States became accustomed to children of color from other countries in its communities, it became easier to accept the transracial adoption of African American children. By 1971 transracial adoptions had reached an annual high of 2,574. Responding to this increase, a 1972 meeting of the National Association of Black Social Workers (NABSW) ended with a resolution opposing transracial adoption:

> Black children belong physically and psychologically and culturally in black families where they can receive the total sense of themselves and develop a sound projection of their future. Only a black family can transmit the emotional and sensitive subtleties of perceptions and reactions essential for a black child's survival in a racist society. Human beings are products of their environment and develop their sense of values, attitudes, and self-concept within their own family structures. Black children in white homes are cut off from the healthy development of themselves as black people.

In response to that resolution, and to the Indian Child Welfare Act of 1978 giving tribal courts exclusive jurisdiction over American Indian child custody proceedings, some states established policies and procedures limiting transracial adoption and requiring that serious efforts be made to place children of color with adoptive parents of their own racial or ethnic group. Agencies specializing in same-race placements were established, and many traditional agencies modified their programs in the same direction.

Criticisms of Protective Policies

Some parents who had adopted transracially were offended, however, by the NABSW resolution, perceiving it as not based in truth and disagreeing with the assertion that they were not capable of parenting their adoptive children of color adequately. White foster parents began to file legal suits to prevent children of color who were in their care from being placed with same-race adoptive parents and to be allowed to adopt the children themselves. Advocates of transracial adoption, some of them transracial adoptive parents themselves, began to speak and write publicly in its support and in opposition to same-race protective policies. Criticism of protective policies for same-race adoption has included the following assertions:

• that same-race placement policies result in retention of children in foster care for longer than necessary, which may result in delay or denial of placement for children of color and therefore in long-term harm . . .

• that agencies apply differential screening criteria to prospective black parents than to prospective white families (such as socioeconomic status, age, and marital status requirements), even though these have not been ruled out as viable criteria for selection

• that empirical studies have been biased toward studying the negative aspects of transracial adoption

• that in spite of such biases, studies have failed to document a negative effect of transracial adoption in areas such as general adjustment and self-esteem and, in some instances, have indicated a possible benefit with regard to the transracial adoptee's ability to get along with and in a white world

• that there is no empirical support for the contention that parents of color do a better job at socializing their children ethnically

• that racial matching policies are in conflict with antidiscrimination legislation, such as the U.S. Constitution and Title IV of the Civil Rights Act of 1964.

A result of the opposition to same-race policies has been that "states have begun to reassess their policies which include race as a viable consideration in placement decision making" [according to the National Coalition to end Racism in America's Child Care System]. . . .

Increase in Transracial Adoptions

The recent increase in transracial adoptions has been influenced by a trend among child welfare agencies toward greater flexibility in eligibility to adopt. Such changes have included less rigidity regarding age, income, housing, family composition, and infertility examination requirements; attempts to make application procedures and agency locations and hours more convenient for prospective adopters; less emphasis on the need for matching the characteristics of child and parent (which may have facilitated same-race placements); a willingness to select single parents or those who already have birth or adopted children; openness to adoption by foster parents, caretakers, and relatives of the child; use of adoption resource exchanges; use of active and ongoing recruitment methods, often using the mass media and featuring specific children; and expansion of adoption subsidy programs. Although some of these changes may facilitate same-race adoptions, they have also opened the way for increases in transracial adoptions. People interested in adopting transracially typically either originally desired a white infant or preschool child and became willing to adopt a child of a different race or were the child's foster parents.

The Multiethnic Placement Act of 1994 prohibited agencies or entities engaged in adoption or foster care placements that receive federal assistance from "categorically deny[ing] to any person the opportunity to become an adoptive or foster parent, solely on the basis of the race, color, or national origin of the adoptive or foster parent or the child" and "from delay[ing] or deny[ing] the placement of a child solely on the basis of race, color, or national origin of the adoptive or foster parent or parents involved." However, this law allowed "an agency or entity to which [the preceding applied to] consider the cultural, ethnic, or racial background of the child and the capacity of the prospective foster or adoptive parents to meet the needs of a child of this background as one of a number of factors used to determine the best interests of a child."

Opponents of same-race protective policies criticized the qualification in the Multiethnic Placement Act that allowed race, culture, and ethnicity to be considered at all and the absence of penalties for failure to conform to the requirements of the act. Advocacy efforts with regard to federal and state adoption policy continued, and in August 1996 legislation was signed that modified the Multiethnic Placement Act of 1994. This legislation, which was enacted as a part of the Small Business Job Protection Act of 1996, had two sections: Section 1807 (Adoption Assistance), which allowed a tax credit to adoptive families with incomes not exceeding $75,000 of up to $5,000 ($6,000 in the case of children with "special needs") annually for qualified adoption expenses, and Section 1808 (Removal of Barriers to Interethnic Adoption), which removed the qualification provided by the earlier act and simply prevented any entity that receives federal funds from denying any person the opportunity to adopt or provide foster care and from delaying or denying the placement of a child on the basis of the race, color, or national origin of the adoptive or foster parent or the child involved. . . .

Given the history of transracial adoption, social workers need to be aware of alternative considerations to those that resulted in the current legislation. Delays in moving children of color out of the out-of-home care system are caused by factors other than restrictions on transracial adoption and can be resolved by actions other than lifting such restrictions. Improvements in six areas would alleviate such delays and lessen the need for transracial adoptions. First, because there are insufficient non-kin foster families of color, policies favoring adoption by foster parents are increasing the numbers of transracial adoptions. Second, there are indications that sufficient numbers of families of color are available to adopt healthy infants of color if such families are sought out and if traditional barriers to adoption are eliminated. Third, many children of color in the child welfare system are not available for adoption or have special needs. Fourth, overrepresentation of children of color in the child welfare system has been linked to disparities in services related to ethnic groups. Fifth, children of color may be counted as being in foster placements when they are actually in permanent kinship care. Finally, poverty, which disproportionately affects families of color, has been associated with the abuse and neglect that often result in the out-of-home placement of children.

Policies Favoring Adoption by Foster Parents

Many children of color are placed with non-kin foster families. [Among California children in one study], only two-thirds of African American children were placed in African American foster homes, and only 31 percent of Hispanic children were placed with Hispanic caregivers. . . . In contrast, 92 percent of selected white children in foster homes were placed with white foster families. The researchers noted that "when children were not placed with ethnically similar foster parents, they were almost always placed with Caucasians [and that] nearly one-half of Caucasian foster parents were caring for children of color."

What has come to be known as the "fost adoption" program emerged in the mid-1970s to promote the placement of children in foster homes with the explicit expectation that the foster parents will adopt the child if reunification with the birth parents fails. Before this program was implemented, foster placements were established in such a way that they would interfere neither with the reunification of the child with her or his birth parents nor with the permanent placement of the child in an adoptive home. Foster parents were considered temporary substitutes, and they were urged not to become attached to the child. If they did become attached, the child was often removed to another placement. With the advent of the "fost adoption" program, white foster families began to seek adoption of children of color placed in their homes, sometimes from birth, even when the children were not placed with the intention of their future adoption by those foster parents.

Thus, insufficient numbers of foster families of color reduce the likelihood that children of color will be adopted by a family of their same racial or ethnic group and gives an advantage to transracial placements. There is evidence that even children of mixed racial parentage tend to be confronted with racism or problems of racial identity while they are in placement, and researchers have recommended that these factors be considered in the selection and preparation of potential foster parents. Increasing the numbers of available foster families of color has the potential, therefore, for increasing same-race adoptive placements. . . .

Availability of Adoptive Families of Color

Evidence indicates that the number of families of color who are willing to adopt healthy infants may be sufficient if agency recruitment and eligibility policies are responsive to the cultures and lifestyles of such families. Early studies documented the failure of adoption agencies to implement culturally sensitive recruitment strategies and eligibility standards for potential adoptees of color. Although many states and agencies took action to correct these circumstances, a recent survey by the North American Council on Adoptable Children found that 83 percent of agencies in the 25 states studied acknowledged that organizational barriers continued to exist that prevented or discouraged families of color from adopting. The most frequently cited barriers were "institutional/systemic racism; lack of people of color in managerial positions; fees; 'adoption as business' mentality; communities' of color historical tendencies toward 'informal' adoption; negative perceptions of agencies and their practices; lack of minority staff; inflexible standards; general lack of recruitment activity and poor recruitment techniques; and 'word not out.'" With regard to the "adoption as business" mentality, one agency head was quoted as saying, "If your agency relied on fees, where would you place a minority kid . . . with a white family that can afford to pay, or a black family that can't?"

When adoption services and programs have become more responsive to families of color, such families have come forward to adopt. . . . Recently, a study by the North American Council on Adoptable Children of 17 agencies specializing in finding same-race adoptive placements for children of color found that these agencies located same-race placements for 94 percent of their 341 African American children and 66 percent of their 38 Hispanic children; nonspecializing agencies obtained an average of 51 percent of same-race placements of 806 African American children and 30 percent of 168 Hispanic children. . . .

Inequities in Services

Disparities related to ethnic group have been observed in the prevention and intervention services that children in the child welfare system receive. The implication is that prevention and intervention services are associated with children's successful exit from the child welfare system, although the authors do not speak directly to this point.

[One author] found that African American children "were more likely to have no contact with workers than were white or Hispanic children." Similarly, African American families studied in the first three months after placement of their children were found to have experienced a mean number of agency contacts of 2.9, compared with a mean of 7.2 for white families. . . .

Kinship Foster Care as Permanent Care

One of the most potentially misleading elements in the argument surrounding children of color in the out-of-home care system is the presentation of foster care statistics. Such statistics seldom distinguish kinship foster placements (placement of dependent children in the homes of relatives who have been formally approved, and subsidized, as foster parents for this purpose) from non-kinship foster placements. This distinction is important. . . . Children of color are widely represented in kinship foster placements. Forty-six percent of selected children in kinship foster care in California were African American, compared with 32 percent white children, 14 percent Hispanic children, and 9 percent children of other ethnic groups. Ninety percent of kinship foster families in a Baltimore study were African American and 10 percent were white. . . .

Effects of Poverty

An overriding issue to be addressed is the circumstances that cause children of color to be in out-of-home placement in such large numbers. Living in poverty is one such circumstance, and it disproportionately affects children of color. Over 46 percent of all African American children lived in poverty in 1993, as did 41 percent of all Latino children; only 14 percent of white children lived in poverty. Fifty-six percent of children living with their mothers only were poor, compared with 12 percent of those living with married parents, and children of color were more likely than white children to live in mother-only households.

"WE ADOPTED."

© Dan Rosandich. Used with permission.

Poverty has been linked to the circumstances that result in out-of-home placements. A recently released National Incidence Study of Child Abuse and Neglect showed that "children from families with annual incomes below $15,000 were over 22 times more likely to experience maltreatment than children from families whose incomes exceeded $30,000. They were also 18 times more likely to be sexually abused, almost 56 times more likely to be educationally neglected, and over 22 times more likely to be seriously injured." Children of single parents had an 87 percent greater risk of being harmed by physical neglect and an 80 percent greater risk of suffering serious injury or harm from abuse and neglect. Thus, children of color may be at greater risk of abuse and neglect, which may be associated with the inadequate resources and resulting stresses their parents confront. Poor children are at risk of permanent removal from their families simply because of their economic position in society.

The direction of public policies currently is to speed up the transracial adoption of children of color without first correcting the resource deficiencies that cause the children to be in out-of-home care. Such policies ignore the complexities of this situation and risk giving one group (those desiring to adopt a young child) an advantage while failing to protect those who are among the most vulnerable (poor children and families). . . .

For a More Responsive Approach

Inequities exist in the eligibility and recruitment of non-kin foster families and adoptive families of color, in services provided to children and families in the child welfare system, and in the increased tendency of poor children to be in out-of-home care. Statistics on the numbers and characteristics of children of color who are in foster care and who are available for adoption may be misleading. Public policies that disallow the consideration of race and ethnicity in adoption give an advantage to families who desire to adopt transracially. At the same time, they fail to correct the circumstances that cause children of color to require out-of-home placement, and they fail to eliminate methods of maintaining or interpreting statistical data that may be misleading.

The following recommendations are made to lessen the need for transracial adoption. First, foster families of color should be actively recruited for kinship and non-kinship foster care and especially to participate in fost adoption programs, if such programs are to continue. Second, active and ongoing efforts to recruit and retain adoptive families of color should be increased so that the pool of available families equals or surpasses the numbers of children of color who are available for non-kin adoption. Third, creative strategies should continue to be developed to recruit adoptive families of color for "hard to place" children or children with special needs. Such children should continue to be placed according to their individual needs. Fourth, public policies and agency procedures should be established to require that children of color receive equitable services in all areas of the child welfare system. Fifth, statistics and outcome data relating to kinship foster care should be separated from those pertaining to nonrelative foster care; the benefits of the former as an acceptable permanent alternative to adoption should be evaluated. And sixth, policymakers should address the larger issues involved in ensuring that all children have access to the economic resources that can help them remain out of the child welfare system. . . .

Seeking to solve the problems associated with the overrepresentation of children of color in the child welfare system by protecting transracial adoption is simplistic and fails to protect those who are most vulnerable in this society—the children dependent on that society.

"Sexual preference should not be the sole criteria on which the suitability of the adoptive parents is based."

Gay and Lesbian Couples Should Have the Right to Adopt

Jill M. Crawford

In the following viewpoint, Jill M. Crawford contends that too many prospective homosexual adoptive couples who can offer children permanent, caring homes are discouraged from adopting by the scrutiny and homophobia they confront during the adoption process. Although single-parent adoption and "loopholes" in existing policies allow some gay and lesbian couples to raise children, she concludes that failing to sanction same-sex couple adoptions denies many children the benefits of having two legally recognized parents. Crawford is an adoption social worker at the Cambridge Family and Children Services in Cambridge, Massachusetts.

As you read, consider the following questions:
1. According to the author, why did one gay couple not pursue adopting Jackie and Todd?
2. What are the two common scenarios in which homosexual couples wish to adopt according to Crawford?
3. What changes does Crawford promote to eliminate adoption policies that discriminate against homosexuals?

Excerpted from "Co-Parent Adoptions by Same-Sex Couples: From Loophole to Law," by Jill M. Crawford, *Families in Society*, vol. 80, no. 3 (May/June 1999), pp. 271–78. Copyright © 1999 Families International Inc. Reprinted with permission.

During my second month employed as an adoption social worker, a case came across my desk that was being assigned to me. Two young brothers, Jackie and Todd, ages six and seven, were in a foster home waiting to be adopted. As usual, I checked to see where the case was being transferred from and why it was being contracted to my agency. At first, what I read puzzled me. It appeared that these boys had had the same social worker for over a year and neither she nor the children were relocating, so I did not understand why there was a change in workers. Further, the "Reason for Referral" slot on the contract was blank. As I read on, things became clearer: an adoptive resource had recently been identified for Jackie and Todd—an upstanding and loving couple with a beautiful home, a lot of energy, and a great big extended family and support network. They sounded too good to be true. Oh, yeah, and they were gay. Apparently the referring agency was having trouble swallowing this bit of information. Once the boys were matched with this couple, the agency that had been working with the children decided that it was "not the appropriate agency to facilitate this adoption," as the proposed outcome was "incompatible with their mission." Thus, the case came to me. . . .

The Big Gap in Our Adoption Policy

Our federal adoption policy, the Adoption Assistance and Child Welfare Act, dates back to 1980. Considered landmark legislation at the time of its inception, today, almost two decades later, it is inadequate, leaving unanswered many questions that have arisen since. The act calls for attempts at family preservation before resorting to substitute care and sets up a mandatory time frame in which various steps of the permanency planning process must be taken, a seemingly aggressive approach. What the law neglects to do, however, is anticipate special issues surrounding adoption or offer guidelines for resolving them. Specifically, the law does not define the concept of "family" and therefore leaves open to interpretation the "appropriateness" of nontraditional families. Since the act was a conservative piece of legislation, it can be assumed that its authors had in mind the conventional nuclear family when thinking about adoption not single parents, blended families, or biracial couples, and certainly not gay men or lesbians. Since there are no guidelines about "suitable" adoptive families, child welfare professionals and court officials are left without direction and consequently impose their own values much of the time. The 1980 act was a family-centered policy, not a child-centered one, and so its efforts were focused on keeping "appropriate" families intact, rather than on the best interests of the children, which may not always be compatible with family preservation. As a result, the law failed to address important adoption-related issues.

Hopes were raised when word spread of a new adoption law, the federal Adoption and Safe Families Act, passed in 1997. Similarly however, it too was of no help in determining who should or should not be granted entrance into this "good-enough-to-adopt" club. Rather, this law's purpose was primarily to accelerate the permanency planning process—an important step, certainly, but still leaving a big gap in our adoption policy. . . .

Under a Microscope

Sadly, Jackie and Todd's adoption by the gay couple fell apart in one of the final stages of the process. The boys were overheard having a conversation of a sexual nature one day (as young boys are prone to do) and alarms went off for this couple. The liability they felt they were walking into with these kids came rushing at them. As a gay couple, they already felt they were "living under a microscope" in their community; add to that two young male children in their care and then the possibility of them making sexual remarks in public, or worse, allegations of sexual abuse against them (as previously traumatized children often do). The couple became acutely aware of how easily their lives could be ruined as a result of the people's misinterpretations—they could lose their home, their jobs, their friends, their dignity . . . and, unfortunately, they were not being unrealistic. This fear compelled them to walk away from the adoption and from two little boys who had grown to love and trust them and who thought they had finally found a family.

We cannot let this happen over and over again. There are

so many children who need families and so many people out there who want to parent them. How, in good conscience, can we deny them each other? The answer is very simple— we can't. We must protect these populations, and all change must begin at the top—with our family policy.

Two scenarios generally exist in which homosexual couples wish to adopt: 1) When one person is the biological parent of the child, and the partner with whom the parent is involved wishes to adopt the child; and 2) when neither partner of the couple is related to the child. The first scenario, called second-parent adoption, can be viewed as similar to stepparent adoption, which has never been viewed as controversial in the context of heterosexual couples. The second, called co-parent adoption, has historically been much more "taboo" and difficult to achieve. . . .

I cannot begin to describe the devastation that the couple's decision to walk away wreaked on Jackie and Todd. The day I had to tell them they were not going to be adopted by this couple after all was, by far, the most difficult task I had ever been faced with. The boys were confused at first, not understanding how I could be breaking all the promises I had made. What had happened to their forever family? Eventually, they turned all that blame inward, viewing themselves as the cause of the failed attempt. Children are inherently egocentric; there is no way they could begin to comprehend the external factors that had led to the disruption. They'd been abandoned before, after all. . . .

Criteria and the Needs of a Child

The gay community has the support of the Child Welfare League of America (CWLA). Their policy is as follows:

> Agencies should assess each applicant from the perspective of what would be in the best interests of the child. The interests of the child are paramount. . . . All applicants should have an equal opportunity to apply for the adoption of children and receive fair and equal treatment and consideration of their qualifications as adoptive parents. . . . Applicants should be fairly assessed on their abilities to successfully parent a child needing family membership and not on their appearance, differing lifestyle, or sexual preference.
>
> Sexual preference should not be the sole criteria on which

the suitability of the adoptive applicants is based. Consideration should be given to other personality and maturity factors and on the ability of the applicant to meet the specific needs of the individual child.

Unfortunately, officers of the court are often uninformed about child welfare issues and their values, which they are forced to rely upon, may be incompatible with the mission of the CWLA.

Six months later, I was contacted by a family that was interested in Jackie and Todd. As coincidence would have it, it was another gay couple. They were from out of state, looking at children in Massachusetts because their home state would not allow them to adopt jointly, and they simply couldn't imagine doing it any other way. . . .

After months of reading and re-reading this couple's homestudy and painstaking team review of their "qualifications," and after countless hours spent on the telephone with Jeff, Scott, and their social worker, we decided to proceed. . . .

Adoption policy in Massachusetts has come a long way this decade, and tremendous gains have been made. The overriding strength of the policy, as it stands, is the unwavering emphasis on the best interests of the child. . . .

The Need for Clear Guidelines

Ironically, that very strength is also a weakness. "Best interests of the child" has become a loosely spoken and vague catch phrase that is not adequately defined anywhere in family policy. We can assume that we all agree that some fundamental needs such as shelter and food must be met in order to serve a child's best interest, but beyond that, it becomes a more subjective matter. People in positions of power certainly are not in consensus on whether gays and lesbians should be allowed to adopt. In an interview with ABC News, Steve Schwalm of the Family Research Council (FRC) stated that gay adoption "knock[s] marriage out of its special status as the proper place for rearing children." Rebecca Biles, also of the FRC, referred to gay adoption as "a loss for children." On the other side of the issue, however, [one author cited by C.S. Cullum] reports research results indicating that "there are no particular developmental or emotional deficits for children raised by gay or lesbian parents." In light of the diversity of views that exist, there is an urgent need for clear guidelines on exactly how to define "best interests." The way the policy is worded now, the court still has the final discretion on whether or not a particular adoption is best for the child. . . .

© Peter Steiner. Used with permission.

There is no specific statement in the policy condoning gay adoption. Therefore, such decisions remain highly contingent on whether or not a judge thinks the adoption is in the best interests of the child. The amount of discretion accorded our judicial system is alarming; yet, current policy does nothing to control for individual opinion. As a result, same-sex couples still need to go to great lengths to prove their parental fitness and, as they spend months and years jumping through hoops and cutting through bureaucratic red tape, children are forced to wait for potentially good families.

A "Special Request"

It was in this next phase that we encountered our first obstacle. Through word-of-mouth, I had learned of an organization that sponsored and paid fully for airplane flights specifically for the purpose of pre-placement visits for interstate adoptions. What luck! We were planning on at least four visits between the children and the couple, and it was getting quite costly. So I eagerly pursued this avenue of free air transportation. At first, they were very accommodating—that is, until they found out the adoption involved a gay couple. The first person I spoke with told me he could not personally handle my request due to personal religous beliefs. He reluctantly offered to pass the request along to someone else. After that, I was stalled for several weeks, given excuses why people weren't returning my calls, and I was generally ignored. Time was growing short, however, so I continued to pester. Finally I was told the request had been referred up to the organization's board of directors. I asked if that was standard procedure and was told that this was "a special request."

I knew what my answer would be long before the official word came down. My request was denied because it was "morally questionable." Words cannot describe how appalled I was at that moment. However, as angry as I was at this organization's audacity to take it upon themselves to rule unfit a family they had never laid eyes on, and as much as I wanted to pursue this matter further, Jeff and Scott said they preferred to spend their energy (and mine) on making the adoption happen as smoothly and quickly as possible. I was amazed at their ability to rise above the discrimination.

Discriminatory Attitudes

The most frightening aspect of that experience was knowing that our laws and policies actually conveyed the same discriminatory attitudes expressed by that organization. The message being sent by our government is that this type of discriminatory behavior is acceptable. Thus, it is clear that some changes need to be made in the policy. First, we need to clarify exactly what the phrase "best interests of the child" means with very specific criteria in order to insulate children from the personal values of our judges and others in powerful decision-making positions. . . .

Second, a clause needs to be added to the policy specifically sanctioning adoption by same-sex couples. This will put an end to any confusion over the existing law and also give gay and lesbian prospective parents the respect they deserve. Their rights should not be manifested in a silly loophole that could be construed as an oversight on the part of policymakers; they should be clearly spelled out for everyone to see and abide by. . . .

Adding to the policy would give indisputable legal recognition to the relationships between a child and both adoptive parents, whereas most current policy only allows a legally binding relationship with one parent. Aside from the emotional and psychological benefits (for both parents and the child) of allowing two partners to jointly petition for adoption, there would also be many more tangible rewards for the child [according to Gay and Lesbian Advocates and Defenders]:

> Because the child is now the legal child of the nonbiological parent [or of both unrelated parents], the child may be entitled to benefits, such as health insurance, that were not previously accessible. Both partners have equal access to medical and school records. . . . If the couple should split up, both partners have the same legal rights to petition for custody and visitation of the child(ren). . . .

If one partner is not legally recognized as the child's parent, he or she has essentially no rights with regard to the child. If the legal parent should predecease the nonlegal parent, the child may be taken from his or her home and placed with relatives or worse, in foster care. There is no reason why a child with two loving parents should ever have to be uprooted like that, especially given the family turmoil he or she has likely been through prior to the adoption. We can offer these children protection by allowing same-sex couples to jointly adopt and by giving both parents' relationships validity by saying so in the policy.

The Most Obvious Barrier

We began pre-placement visits (thanks to commercial airlines and funding from the Department of Social Services), and the transition could not have gone better. Jackie and Todd were slow to trust, of course—they'd been burned before. But that would come with time. Today, the adoption is moving along without a hitch. The children have moved in with their new family and are doing beautifully. Of course, they will have to return to Massachusetts to legalize the adoption in six months, since their own state of residence will not recognize both men as legal parents—one last barrier just to remind them that they are different. . . .

Unfortunately, today's society poses many obstacles to implementing the above changes, despite the clear advantages of doing so. The biggest and most obvious barrier to change is persistent homophobia. This is not surprising considering that homosexuality was defined by the *Diagnostic and Statistical Manual of Mental Disorders* as a form of mental illness until 1973. Although that stigma was nominally lifted twenty-five years ago, deeply instilled values are difficult to change. Regarding adoption specifically, [Andrew Sullivan said,]

> The judgment and beliefs of the general public are often clouded by three misperceptions or myths: 1) children might be molested by homosexual adoptive parents; 2) children will become gay or be pressured to become gay if they are placed in homosexual adoptive families; and 3) children adopted by homosexuals will be living in an "immoral" environment.

The first two of these myths have been disproved in numerous research studies, and the third is a highly subjective issue, wide open to individual interpretation. Unfortunately, it is often personal opinion and not empirical data that shapes our policies. . . .

For the Sake of Children

Meanwhile, Jackie and Todd have barely noticed that they are in the minority, having two dads instead of a mother and a father. What is so much more important to them is that they finally have the forever family they have dreamed about for so long. Certainly they will have questions and concerns about having gay parents as they grow older. But with parents like Jeff and Scott, who are comfortable with themselves, articulate about their situation, and supportive of their children, this family will continue to rise above society's prejudices for as long as they have to. Hopefully, the winds of change will blow before these children grow old enough to understand what discrimination is and become ashamed of the world in which they live.

In times of moral crisis, as our policymakers and child welfare professionals must often feel, it is helpful to heed the words of Justice Brennan from a 1989 Massachusetts Supreme Court decision:

> We are not an assimilative, homogeneous society, but a facilitative, pluralistic one, in which we must be willing to abide by someone else's unfamiliar or even repellent practice because the same tolerant impulse protects our own idiosyncrasies. Even if we agree, therefore, that "family" and "parenthood" are part of the good life, it is absurd to assume that we can agree on the content of those terms and destructive to pretend that we do.

The question then, is, what can be done to create a less-threatening arena in which gay people can adopt? One thing is clear: We cannot change the children. Unfortunately, children "of the system" will always be traumatized in one way or another; and we, as professionals, cannot guarantee that those kids will never act out inappropriately as a result. In fact, we can almost guarantee that they will. We know for a fact that child sexual abuse survivors tend to have a repertoire of sexually charged behaviors. We also know that "normal" children, i.e., those who have never been sexually abused, will eventually become curious about sex and act out that curiosity in any number of developmentally appropriate ways. It is practically an inevitable milestone on the path to adolescence.

How then can the fear and frustration felt by that first couple and, I will assume, many others, be eradicated? We cannot change the children (at least not in any immediate way), and we cannot change a couple's "gayness." The only area we can improve upon, it seems, is societal misperception and prejudice. The deep-seated fear and hatred of gays so rampant in our society, which is perpetuated by the myths previously discussed, has attached itself to our child welfare system like a parasite and is quickly draining the life—the spirit, the goodness, the energy, and the genuineness—from our pool of prospective parents whom we so desperately need. It simply has to stop; for the sake of the children, we must stop it.

> *"Some of the research suggests that there are some serious potential harms to children raised by homosexual parents."*

Gay and Lesbian Parenting May Not Be Beneficial

Lynn D. Wardle

Lynn D. Wardle is a professor of law at the J. Reuben Clark Law School at Brigham Young University and author of various publications concerning same-sex marriage and children's rights. In the following viewpoint, he argues that homosexual parenting may harm children. According to Wardle, homosexual relationships, like all extramarital sexual relationships, are detrimental to the emotional well-being of children. Children of homosexual parents are more likely to engage in homosexual behavior and experience various emotional and social conflicts. Therefore, he concludes, homosexual parenting—including adoption by gays and lesbians—should not be legally sanctioned.

As you read, consider the following questions:
1. According to Wardle, how is the current legal literature on homosexual parenting flawed?
2. In the author's opinion, what three sampling flaws affect the results of most homosexual parenting studies?
3. How does Wardle counter the argument that a homosexual couple can provide for a child better than a single parent?

Excerpted from "The Potential Impact of Homosexual Parenting on Children," by Lynn D. Wardle, *University of Illinois Law Review*, no. 3 (1997). Copyright © 1997 The Board of Trustees of the University of Illinois. Reprinted by permission.

The proposed restructuring of the family to legitimate homosexual family relations may be among the most heavily advocated family law reforms to be discussed in recent years. For example, a year ago I reviewed as much of the law review literature as I could find on the subject of same-sex marriage that had been published between January 1990 and December 1995. I found seventy-two articles, notes, comments, and essays about same-sex marriage published in law reviews available in North America, a nine-fold increase over the eight law review pieces on the same subject published in a similar period two decades earlier, when the topic was first seriously raised in litigation in the United States. There has been a similar explosion in the law review literature advocating the legalization of what I will herein call homosexual parenting—that is, the exercise of unrestricted, unconditional parental relationship rights, fully equivalent to those enjoyed by heterosexual parents, by lesbian and gay couples, homosexual biological or adoptive parents, homosexual partners and ex-partners of biological parents, and homosexual prospective legal parents (homosexual individuals seeking to adopt children or become parents by means of assisted procreation). At least ninety different law review articles, comments, notes, or essay pieces primarily addressing custody, visitation, assisted procreation, and adoption issues involving gay or lesbian parents have been published since 1990, compared to only three pieces published in the same period twenty years earlier. . . .

The legalization of homosexual parenting, essentially rendering sexual conduct of a parent a presumably irrelevant factor for purposes of child custody, visitation, and other child welfare cases, would constitute a significant shift in the legal and social assumptions and legal model of parenting. Accordingly, the proposals to legalize same-sex marriage and homosexual parenting certainly should be thoroughly and carefully considered. Likewise, the legalization of same-sex marriage would represent profound alteration of the structure of marriage and the family. That, of course, is where the law review literature plays an important role. Historically, lawyers have distinguished themselves by their ability to take all sides in the debate of proposed legal reforms, and law reviews have excelled in providing a forum for the "free trade in ideas," the "robust debate of public issues" that is essential to our system of free government. The current generation of law review literature, however, fails to provide that important function with respect to the same-sex marriage and homosexual parenting issues. The current literature fails to provide almost any serious criticism, scrutiny, or even a modest exchange of opposing opinions. In the law reviews, the "broad dissemination of principles, ideas, and factual information . . . [and] robust public debate" that is needed to test and refine the proposal has not even begun. . . .

Most of the articles advocating homosexual parenting are filled with adult-rights talk. Although this certainly is a legitimate perspective, in this area of law (dealing with doctrines and policies protecting and promoting parent-child relations), it probably is not the most important focus. The focus on the welfare of children and the social interests in the parent-child relation ought to be central, and the adult-rights focus secondary. Yet much of the law review literature is clearly adult-advocacy literature attempting to vindicate a particular rule or principle for the benefit of a certain class of adults. The manipulation of child-oriented rules of law for the political purposes and benefits of adults is troubling. . . .

Methodological and Sampling Flaws

The publication of studies of homosexual parenting in social science literature has dramatically increased in recent years. Like scientific reports purporting to find biological origins for homosexual behavior (gay genes, brain structures, etc.), most of the recently published social science studies about homosexual parenting are highly affirming of persons in homosexual relationships. They purport to show that childrearing by homosexual parents is equivalent to (as beneficial for children as), if not superior to, childrearing by heterosexual parents. Studies are cited in the law review literature as proof that the homosexual behavior or relationship of parents has no detrimental effect on parenting skills or on children raised by such parents. Likewise, the case law relies heavily, and often excessively, upon studies purporting to show that homosexual parenting is functionally equivalent to heterosexual parenting and not harmful to children. Because of substantial methodological and analytical flaws, however, the studies do not provide a reliable basis for such conclusions. . . .

The first methodological problem with many of the studies of the effect of parental homosexual behavior on children or childrearing is small sample size. In order to provide any conclusions that provide statistically reliable predictive data that would be valid for policy making, the samples must be of significant numerical size. For example, a recent study of the effect of certain "at risk" factors on the welfare of children involved a survey of 34,129 children from an initial sample of 250,000 surveys taken in 460 communities in thirty-two states. None of the studies of parenting by adults engaged in homosexual relationships is of comparable size or reliability. Most of the studies of childrearing by parents in homosexual relationships involve samples of a few dozen, frequently as few as ten to forty subjects—the studies of Charlotte Patterson, the most prominent producer and advocate of this literature, for example—and some studies use sample populations as small as five. The studies of such small sample populations do not provide reliable quantitative research conclusions about parenting or child development.

Another sampling flaw in many of the studies cited to show the lack of harm to children of gay or lesbian parenting is the reliance on the "sample of convenience." Many of the studies involve subjects who are self-selected, or at least not randomly selected, such as subjects "recruited through advertisements in homophile publications." Volunteers for such studies often have an interest in the outcome of the study that distorts the research. Thus, the sample population in these studies is not likely to fairly represent the whole group of homosexual parents that is to be examined. The assertiveness and zeal of self-selected sample populations may not fairly represent the population sought to be sampled. . . .

Another sampling flaw concerns the control groups with which the homosexual parents and their children are compared. Seldom are married heterosexual families used as comparisons. Often the control groups consist of single heterosexual parents and their children. This results in comparison of a favorably composed group of homosexual parents and children with a control group drawn from the segment of the heterosexual parent-child population that is most disadvantaged. . . .

Effects on the Child's Sexual Development

Given the sympathetic orientation and methodological bias of the social science studies of the effects of homosexual parenting on children, it is remarkable that the data reported in some of these studies provides a basis for serious concerns about potential detrimental effects upon children raised by gay or lesbian parents. Because of the methodological flaws mentioned above (such as small sample size), the concerns cannot be called conclusive, but the data certainly raise questions that need to be examined. Until these concerns are conclusively dispelled, it would not be rational to adopt a public policy endorsing or legitimating homosexual parenting. The most obvious risk to children from their parents' homosexual behavior suggested by the current studies relates to the sexual development of the child. Both theory and empirical studies indicate the potential that disproportionate percentages of children raised by homosexual parents will develop homosexual interests and behaviors. . . .

One published case report suggests a link between a daughter's sexual behavior and fantasy and her mother's homosexual behavior: the daughter in the reported case study had experimented with homosexual practices and also indulged in heterosexual promiscuity, anxiously driven by her awareness of her mother's homosexual relations. Another study of New York children reared by lesbian mothers (mostly in couples) and those reared by divorced homosexual single mothers suggested that "[t]here is a possibility that rearing [by a homosexual parent] might influence [the child's] sexual partner choice, temporarily or permanently." [Ghazala] Javaid also observed that "a girl in a lesbian home could be more vulnerable [to developing homosexual attraction] because of an increased awareness of herself in relation to other women and a sensitivity to environmental prejudices such as 'the daughter of a gay woman could be gay herself'" and acknowledged that "the effect of an additional exposure to [the lesbian] subculture" might "promote internalized permission for homosexual behaviour." Javaid's study found that four of the twenty-six children raised by lesbian mothers were "asexual" compared to none of the twenty-eight children raised by heterosexual single mothers. Four of the children raised by lesbian mothers stated that they did not want to have children, compared to none of the children raised by heterosexual single mothers. Three of the thirteen lesbian mothers preferred for their daughters to become homosexual, compared to none of the fifteen heterosexual single mothers, and all of the heterosexual mothers (100%) hoped their children would marry and have children, but only nine of thirteen lesbian mothers (69%) wanted their children to have children. Although far from definitive and too small to provide reliable conclusions, this study clearly suggests that homosexual parenting may have some effect upon children in relation to the whole constellation of developmental issues surrounding their own sexuality. One critical report reviewed three reports that found homosexual orientation in approximately nine percent to twelve percent of children raised by homosexual parents and noted: "These three summaries of the literature—by three different teams of investigators—agree in stating that homosexual parents appear to produce a disproportionate percentage of bisexual and homosexual children." Indeed, one sympathetic review of the literature candidly acknowledged that "Clinical studies do suggest a number of possible areas in which the mother's sexual identity might be an issue for the children.". . .

Other "Noticeable" Concerns

Increased likelihood of homosexual interest is not the only potential risk for children raised by homosexual parents. Javaid's study also discovered "noticeable" concerns for both lesbian mothers and their sons regarding discipline, expectations, and general parent-child relations. Other studies have also reported that boys raised by homosexual mothers may have a lower self-image regarding masculinity. Children born to or adopted by lesbian mothers who were examined by Charlotte Patterson, for example, showed more symptoms of stress and were "more likely to report feeling angry, scared or upset." A study of children of lesbians by Karen Gail Lewis revealed a "defensiveness" on the part of the children of lesbian couples she studied, a pattern of denial—especially deep in the youngest child in the lesbian couples she studied, hostility from older boys, especially directed at the mother's lesbian lover, children's expressed concern for the welfare of siblings, children's concerns about their own sexuality, children's concerns about the integrity of their family, concerns about their mother's homosexual activities, evidence that one of the lesbian mothers expressly encouraged her daughters to make lesbian sexual choices, children forced to conceal one parent's secret sexual behaviors from the other parent, and "gross maladaptive behavior [by older teenagers that] occurred around the time of the mother's disclosure [of her lesbian relationship]." Studies biased in favor of homosexual parenting disclosed that children (especially daughters) of lesbians have increased levels of fantasized anxiety, increased tendencies toward inhibition, increased tendencies toward sadness (at least sons of lesbians), and disclosed increased cross-dressing among daughters, and less cooperative behavior. Sons of lesbians were reportedly more influenced by peers than children raised by heterosexual parents.

Extramarital Sexual Relations

Finally, it is reasonable to be concerned that ongoing parental homosexual sexual behavior is harmful to children because that seems to be the lesson of the most relevant and analogous human experience—the experience of extramarital sexual relations generally. The standard and expectation that responsible sexual relations must occur within the heterosexual marriage relationship is deeply rooted in our society and legal system. Extramarital sexual behavior is associated with such harm to children as the breakup of their parents' marriage and the destabilizing, child-harming consequences of divorce. Parental extramarital relationships wound children, shaking, sometimes even destroying, their faith in marriage and in personal commitments of fidelity and intimacy. It hurts a child to learn that one parent has been unfaithful to the other. That pain is very real and very wrenching. Parental extramarital relationships also provide a dangerous model for children, serving to pass intergenerational self-destructive behavior on to children. The message of intergender and intergenerational carelessness, and family-sacrificing selfishness not only hurts, but also may have a programming effect on children. The lesson of sexual self-gratification at the expense of familial fidelity conveys a tragic message about both family commitments and responsible sexual behavior in our society. In these days of so many harmful, even deadly, sexually transmitted diseases, the risks may be physical as well as emotional.

Reprinted by permission of Chuck Asay and Creators Syndicate, Inc.

The potential harm to children from homosexual behavior of their parents, however, should not be exaggerated. First, many of the studies are not of large sample populations and have other methodological deficiencies. Moreover, the reasons that men and women turn to homosexual relationships are many and complex, and do not necessarily or always cancel or override their love for and commitment to their children. Some parents with homosexual orientation undoubtedly are very committed to the welfare of their children, and the kinds of potential risks that may be associated with homosexual parenting may not differ significantly from those associated with heterosexual parenting by adults who engage in heterosexual extramarital activity. Nevertheless, although the social science research is not conclusive, it does suggest that there are some particular and unique potential risks to children raised by active homosexual parents.

The Advantages of Dual-Gender Parenting

Children raised by homosexual couples do not have both a father and a mother. If Heather is being raised by two mommies only, she is being deprived of the experience of being raised by a daddy. Both the common experience of humanity and recent research suggest that a daddy and a mommy together provide by far the best environment in which a child may be reared.

Among the most important reasons why heterosexual parenting is best for children is because there are gender-linked differences in child-rearing skills; men and women contribute different (gender-connected) strengths and attributes to their children's development. Although the critical contributions of mothers to the full and healthy development of children has long been recognized, recent research validates the common understanding that fathers, as well as mothers, are extremely important for child development.

Experts in many disciplines that have recently been studying fathering have reached "surprising unanimity" in their recognition that "[m]en nurture, interact with, and rear competently but differently from women: not worse, not better . . . differently." When fathers nurture and care for their children, they do so not quite as "substitute mothers" but differently, as fathers. For example, some studies show that fathers play with their infant children more than mothers, play more physical and tactile games than mothers, and use fewer toys when playing with their children. Mothers tend to talk and play more gently with infant children. Compared to mothers, fathers reportedly appear to "have more positive perceptions of the more irritable sons and less irritable daughters," and perceive their baby daughters to be more cuddly than mothers do. Mothers smile and verbalize more to the infant than fathers do, and generally rate their infant sons as cuddlier than fathers do. Moreover, "[m]en encouraged their children's curiosity in the solution of intellectual and physical challenges, supported the child's persistence in solving problems, and did not become overly solicitous with regard to their child's failures." One study found that six-month-old infants whose fathers were actively involved with them "had higher scores on the Bailey Test of Mental and Motor Development." Infants whose fathers spend more time with them are more socially responsive and better able to withstand stressful situations than infants relatively deprived of substantial interaction with their fathers. . . .

Parents are important as role models for their children of the same gender because "[c]hildren learn to be adults by watching adults." Children are generally more compliant with the parent of the same sex. The importance of the opposite-gendered parent for the complete emotional and social development of the child is now recognized as well: "Boys and girls build their notions of their sex roles from experience with both sexes." The loss of cross-gender parenting may have severe emotional consequences for the child. For example, the absence of a father in the home may result in a daughter having trouble relating to men throughout her adult life. . . .

The Most Profound Advantage

Among the most profound advantages of marriage is basic economic security for children. Marital status is more closely associated with avoiding child poverty than any other factor. One study reported that more than half of the increase in child poverty in the United States between 1980 and 1988 "can be accounted for by changes in family structure during the 1980s." In addition, "[c]hanging family structure also accounted for 48 percent of the increase during the 1980s in deep poverty, and 59 percent of the rise in relative poverty among U.S. children." Many studies have shown that children in single-parent families are many times more likely to be living in poverty than children living with both a mother and father. William Galston, who served as a Domestic Policy Advisor to President Clinton, agreed that "[i]t is no exaggeration to say that a stable, two-parent family is an American child's best protection against poverty." Thus, "[a]s a matter of public policy, if not of morality, it pays for society to approve of marriage as the best setting for children."

Advocates of homosexual parenting may argue that two homosexuals could provide for a child economically better than a single parent. However, any overall economic benefit could be more than offset by the overall economic costs and chronic instability of homosexual liaisons, especially gay liaisons. Concerns about the welfare of children have caused the Scandinavian countries with legalized homosexual domestic partnerships to deny to same-sex couples all rights of adoption, including domestic adoptions and even stepparent adoptions, as well as rights of joint custody (in Denmark and Sweden) and assisted procreation. Homosexual parenting poses particular risks for the emotional and gender development of children. Children make the transition through developmental stages better, have stronger gender identity, are more confident of themselves, do better in school, have fewer emotional crises, and become functioning adults best when they are reared in two-parent, dual-gender families. . . .

Same-Sex Partnerships and Children's Rights

It is possible to justify legalization of some marriage-like status for same-sex couples without extending marriage-like benefits relating to childrearing. In the past eight years, four independent Scandinavian nations, Denmark, Norway, Sweden, and Iceland, have legalized same-sex domestic partnerships, extending to those registered relationships virtually all of the economic incidents of heterosexual marriage. However, those permissive laws are quite restrictive with regard to childrearing rights. The Icelandic law specifically excludes same-sex couples from adoption and artificial insemination. In Denmark, the same-sex couple may not adopt a child or exercise joint custody. The Swedish law excludes adoption, joint custody, and fertilization in vitro for registered same-sex domestic partnerships. In Norway, same-sex registered partnerships may not adopt.

All of these countries manifest a permissive policy concerning relations between two consenting adults, but all take a paternalistic posture when it comes to protecting children. The common theme is that adults can do what they want with regard to other consenting adults, but they are not free to do whatever they want with regard to children. These nations take great care to prevent adults from subjecting children to the potentially detrimental effects and consequences of adult sexual preferences. Although homosexual behavior may not bar a responsible biological parent from asserting parental rights—consistent, again, with the permissive non-judgmental attitude about adult behavior—the Scandinavian states put the needs and interests of the children ahead of the autonomy rights of adults. Several years ago, Mary Ann Glendon demonstrated that in many ways in family law, European nations manifest a much greater care and protection for children than the laws of the United States. The Scandinavian laws extending legal benefits to same-sex domestic partnerships but restricting adoption, joint custody, and assisted procreation by those couples seem to manifest that distinctive concern for children. . . .

Premature and Unwise

The social science literature that is cited in support of the claim that homosexual parenting is not significantly harmful to children is unreliable. Methodological defects and analytical flaws abound in the studies. The research is colored significantly by bias in favor of homosexual parenting. Despite the favorable gloss put on the data, some of the research suggests that there are some serious potential harms to children raised by homosexual parents. . . .

It would be premature and unwise to legalize homosexual parenting by extending full, unrestricted, parental relationship rights to homosexual parents equivalent to those of heterosexual parents. Legalization of same-sex marriage would be unwise for many of the same reasons. The impact upon children of such radical changes in the form and structure of the family and in the institution of marriage that is the basis of the family, and of society, have not been carefully considered.

Children are the innocent victims who suffer the most from choices their parents make to experiment for personal self-gratification with extramarital sexual relationships. We must be concerned that a parent who makes a calculated decision to deprive a child of a parent of the opposite gender may be making a decision that shows insufficient regard for the needs of children. As Dame Mary Warnock wrote in her committee's celebrated report on artificial conception technology: "[w]e believe that as a general rule it is better for children to be born into a two-parent family, with both father and mother, although we recognize that it is impossible to predict with any certainty how lasting such a relationship will be." In an important sense, the question whether homosexual parenting should be legitimated ultimately depends on what kind of society we want our children and grandchildren to grow up in. Parental fidelity to the relationship that generated a child, to the partnership that produced the child, is a powerfully positive influence in the life of the child. If we want to put children's needs first, we must preserve for them the basic social institution which has over the millennia been the most beneficial of all imperfect human institutions for children's welfare. Thus, we should think very carefully before accepting the invitation to legitimate the brave new world of homosexual parenting as a desirable environment in which to rear future generations.

Periodical Bibliography

The following articles have been selected to supplement the diverse views presented in this chapter. Addresses are provided for periodicals not indexed in the *Readers' Guide to Periodical Literature*, the *Alternative Press Index*, the *Social Sciences Index*, or the *Index to Legal Periodicals and Books*.

Scott Baldauf	"How Texas Wrestles with Gay Adoptions," *Christian Science Monitor*, December 3, 1997.
Mei Griebenow	"Looking Chinese Adoption in the Eyes," *In the Family*, Spring 2000. Available from Family Magazine, Inc., 7302 Hilton Ave., Takoma Park, MD 20912.
Marilyn Johnson	"What Happens to Children Nobody Wants? Sometimes They End Up With an Elderly Blind Woman," *Life*, May 1997.
Anne Adams Lang	"When Parents Adopt a Child and a Whole Other Culture," *New York Times*, March 8, 2000.
Tara Mack	"The Export of American Babies," *Ladies' Home Journal*, October 2000.
Amanda T. Perez	"Transracial Adoption and the Federal Law Subsidy," *Yale Law and Policy Review*, 1998.
Scott D. Ryan	"Examining Social Workers' Placement Recommendations of Children With Gay and Lesbian Adoptive Parents," *Families in Society: Journal of Contemporary Human Services*, September 2000. Available from Manticore Publishers, PO Box 711, Lewiston, NY 14092.
Eric Schmidtt	"Children Adopted Abroad Win Automatic Citizenship: Law Ends a Costly and Protracted Process," *New York Times*, February 22, 2001.
Lynn N. Tauer	"The Cost of Single Parent Adoptions," *Adoptive Families*, January/February 1996. Available from Adoptive Families, 2472 Broadway, Suite 377, New York, NY 10025.
Steven L. Varnis	"Regulating the Global Adoption of Children," *Society*, January 2001.
Cheryl Wetzstein	"Adoption Survey Records Slight Dip: Special Needs Cases Double in Decade," *Washington Times*, November 24, 1999.

CHAPTER 4

Should Adoption Policies Be Changed?

Chapter Preface

In 2000, Tina Johnson, a San Diego-based Internet adoption broker, exploited two hopeful adoptive couples. After Johnson had placed Kiara and Keyara, a pair of twin baby girls, with Richard and Vickie Allen, their birth mother took them back and gave them to Alan and Judith Kilshaw, a British couple that offered Johnson a higher fee for the twins. The Kilshaws then flew to Arkansas, adopted the babies under the state's lenient adoption laws, and renamed them Kimberley and Belinda.

When Johnson's scam was revealed, an Arkansas judge nullified the adoption on the grounds that the Kilshaws did not meet the state's residency requirements. In addition, the Allens had not lived with the children long enough to make a legal claim their custody. Without any legal guardians, Kimberely and Belinda were placed in foster care.

This Internet adoption scandal prompted many critics to oppose using the Internet to facilitate adoptions. Some critics argue that adoption brokers and lawyers use chat rooms and e-mail to target couples who are desperate to adopt. To others, Internet adoption encourages an underground market of baby-selling. Reporter Cheah Chor Sooi comments, "Belinda and Kimberley are only two of hundreds of babies sold daily worldwide through the various web sites."

However, others support the use of the Internet to match children with available families. In the words of adoption.com, a web-based adoption organization, "The Internet has provided the opportunity to reach individuals who wish for their lives to be touched by adoption." Some proponents add that the Internet adoption scandal simply reveals the need for federal regulations on adoption. "One big problem," says adoption facilitator Ellen Roseman, "is that every state has different laws."

The case of the Internet twins renewed debates about adoption laws and policies. The following chapter presents the arguments on how new laws and policies may affect adoption and whether or not these changes are necessary.

"Open adoption . . . is not a solution to the problems inherent in adoption."

Adoption with Clear Familial Boundaries Is Best

Mary Beth Seader and William L. Pierce

Open adoption is intended to ease the grief of separation by allowing the birth mother to establish an ongoing relationship with her child. In the following viewpoint, Mary Beth Seader and William L. Pierce oppose this practice and contend that open adoption may actually prolong or worsen the birth mother's pain. The authors claim that when the birth mother is allowed to continually contact her child, it inhibits her from defining the loss and achieving closure. Seader serves on the board of directors for the National Council for Adoption (NCFA), an adoption advocacy and child welfare organization. Pierce founded the NCFA, formerly served as its president, and is executive editor of *The Adoption Factbook*.

As you read, consider the following questions:

1. In the authors' opinion, why are many birth mothers of adopted children "stuck" in the grieving process?
2. According to Kathleen Silber and Patricia Martinez Dorner, how can open adoption interrupt the bonding process between adoptive parents and their child?
3. According to Seader and Pierce, what may happen when a young child is made aware that he or she has a birth mother?

From "Parent Access After Adoption: Should Parents Who Give Up Their Children for Adoption Continue to Have Access to Them? No," by Mary Beth Seader and William L. Pierce, in *Debating Children's Lives*, edited by Mary Ann Mason and Eileen Gambrill, pp. 26–31. Copyright © 1994 by Sage Publications, Inc. Reprinted by permission of Sage Publications, Inc.

The way the question is phrased—"Should parents who give up their children for adoption continue to have access to them?"—reminds one of how pollsters can get very different responses from the same group of people just by asking the same question in different ways. The question evokes an immediate emotional response. The phrases "give up" and "have access" make it sound as though a parent has made a self-centered decision that she does not want the responsibilities of being a parent, but wants to continue the benefits of the relationship. In that respect, denying access would be seen as a punishment for the "crime" of "giving up" the child. This is not what the discussion about "open" adoption or "openness" in adoption is about today.

The question about whether there should be continued contact between women and men who have planned adoption and adopted persons must be addressed in terms of the possible risks and benefits of the contact for all parties, but particularly the child. The catalyst for the practice of continued contact in adoption came from reports by women who had placed children for adoption; those women said that they felt unresolved grief over adoptions that had occurred many years before.

An Unenforceable Agreement

Since the 1970s, when the idea first began to emerge, the movement for open adoption has taken on a life of its own for a variety of reasons. As practitioners who had observed some birth parents (mostly women) who had placed children for adoption and who unquestionably had unresolved grief began to write and speak on the problems of this clinical population, they began to attract others who reported problems of women who had placed, until some in the field of adoption universalized the experience of these women to all women who placed children for adoption. Open adoption was proposed as the solution, but open adoption did not "fix" the problems of unresolved grief, as evidenced by the words of Reuben Pannor and Annette Baran, who now say that "relinquishment of children to a new set of parents, as a final, irrevocable act, severing all rights of the birth parents, must be discontinued. Open adoption, which we helped pioneer, is not a solution to the problems inherent in adoption. Without legal sanction, open adoption is an unenforceable agreement at the whim of the adoptive parent. Instead a form of guardianship adoption would be in the best interest of all concerned." What Pannor and Baran and others have proposed is that adoption be restructured, so that it looks more like foster care.

It is our contention that proponents of open adoption have misdiagnosed the problem; therefore, their solution not only does not address the problem, but in many cases exacerbates the problem. First, proponents of open adoption conclude that it is the separation that causes the problem. It is a fact that loss causes pain. However, it is not a fact that individuals cannot recover from loss. Life is a series of losses, and if individuals could not recover from them, this would be a planet of basket cases. It is a fact that some individuals have more trouble than others in resolving losses, for a variety of reasons, including previous life experiences, individual capacity (which may be affected by stage of development and other factors), and social supports. It is also a reality that a "problem pregnancy" itself is a crisis that precipitates losses, regardless of the decision made about how to manage the pregnancy. The role of the counselor is not to deny or obliterate the loss, but to support the client through the loss to a healthy resolution. This does not mean that the individual will forget about the loss, or that there will not be some regrets and moments of pain. Reaching a healthy resolution means that the individual can go on to lead a peaceful, happy, productive life.

Our personal experiences as counselors and a review of the literature indicate that women who have placed children for adoption who continue to experience pain from the experience have become "stuck" in the grieving process. Often what emerges is an inability to forgive themselves for getting into the situation to begin with and for not being prepared to parent. There is also often an inability to forgive the father of the baby, family, friends, and society for not providing more support, and the adoption worker and agency as representative of the source of the pain.

In her book *Saying Goodbye to a Baby*, Patricia Roles, advocate of open adoption, describes the common grief reaction of "searching behavior" (which may range from scanning crowds for babies to all-out attempts to make contact with the adopted child) as generally part of the "anger phase" of mourning. The anger, which is often very intense, prevents the woman who placed her child from forgiving, which is necessary for a peaceful resolution. Unless the woman can let go of the anger, she cannot move forward to the final stage of acceptance and peace.

So what can continued access to their children do to help women who are going through this grieving process? Common sense and an understanding of grieving theory suggest, not much. The searching behavior is an attempt to undo the loss. Continued contact, or open adoption, is also an attempt to undo the loss. The reality of adoption is that the person who places the child ceases to be the parent, and continued contact can be very confusing to the person who placed the child and the child's family. Continued contact inhibits the grieving process because it makes it difficult to define the loss and therefore have closure.

Remaining Frozen

Carole Anderson, president of Concerned United Birthparents (CUB), an advocacy group for people who have placed children for adoption and who have had negative experiences, agrees with Pannor and Baran that open adoption has not resolved the problem. She writes, "The way most open adoptions are handled, with birthparents participating in their own destruction and suffering from more ambiguous losses, it may be even harder for open adoption birthparents to acknowledge and face their losses. . . . these birthparents seem to remain in a frozen, childlike state for very long periods."

A study at the University of Texas at Arlington on the postadoptive grief experience of women who had placed children for adoption found that

> indications were strong that biological mothers who know more about the later life of the child they relinquished have a harder time making an adjustment than do mothers whose tie to the child is broken off completely by means of death. Relinquishing mothers who know only that their children still live but have no details about their lives appear to experience an intermediate degree of grief.

Blending Birth with Adopting Families

Open adoption provides no seal of confidentiality regarding the identity of the birth parents, the adopting parents, and the child. It essentially blends birth families with adopting families, directly undermining the creation of a permanent new family for a child. The professional literature shows a frequent confusion of roles when the birth family continues a relationship with the child. This also interferes with parent and child bonding in the adoptive family and inhibits the birth parents' grieving process. There are parallel experiences and research findings with respect to divorce and the increased risks of being raised in blended families. Confidentiality, especially in infant adoptions, helps minimize these risks.

Patrick F. Fagan, *Heritage Foundation Backgrounder,* July 27, 1995.

There is mounting evidence that open adoption has not addressed the needs of the people who place, and there are increasing complaints that adoptive parents are not fulfilling agreements for contact they made prior to the adoption finalization, indicating that open adoption arrangements have not been satisfactory for adoptive families. There are efforts in some states to pass legislation requiring adoptive parents to comply with prefinalization agreements for contact. One could argue that this interferes with the adoptive parents' rights and responsibilities as the legal and moral parents to the child. This is precisely what Pannor and Baran refer to when they say that open adoption does not go far enough in maintaining the rights of people who place, because in adoption, the adoptive parents are more than guardians, they are the full parents, for all intents and purposes, of the child. Adoption was created out of the recognition that children need to feel secure about who their parents are and what their role is. If adoption professionals are candid, they will make sure that all people who place understand this completely before they consent to adoption.

Interfering with Adoptive Parents' Roles

So it would appear that open adoption does not reach its intended goal of relieving any pain resulting from a "problem pregnancy" and adoption for the person who places. And if it creates problems for the adoptive family because it interferes with the parents' role as parents to the child, what effect does it have on the child? Kathleen Silber and Patricia Martinez Dorner, in their book *Children of Open Adoption*, report:

> During this honeymoon period [after the placement of the child], it is important for the adoptive parents to have some "space." That is, they need time (without interference by the birthmother) to bond with the baby and establish their own intimate relationship as a family. If there is too frequent contact with the birthmother during these first few weeks, the couple can over-identify with her and her pain, thereby continuing to view the baby as "her baby."

Young Children Do Not Understand Adoption

Silber and Dorner wrote *Children of Open Adoption* to show the "positive" effects of open adoption on children who have been involved. Because open adoption is a fairly new concept as currently practiced, the study was limited to children under the age of 9 or 10. The authors report that the children respond positively to and show genuine affection for the parents who placed them for adoption. Given the nature of children, one would expect that children would respond positively to caring adults. However, Silber and Dorner seem to take great leaps when they discuss children's understanding and acceptance of adoption and their birth parents: "As Alberta Taubert indicates, her three-year-old daughter, Jordan, is able to appropriately use the term birthmother and to realize that she grew in Christy's womb and, in fact, got her curly hair from Christy. Of course, Jordan only has an elementary understanding of adoption." A child of 3 calling a woman "birth mother" does not indicate that she understands the relationship. Certainly, the authors do not expect the readers to believe that a 3-year-old has an understanding of genetics and the transmission of "curly" genes.

Silber and Dorner say that in their work with children of open adoption they found that

> the realization and experience of loss is demonstrated by adopted children at earlier ages than previously believed. The different manifestations of grief are evidenced by the children—we see denial, sadness, and anger. Jennifer's story reflects how denial came into play for this child. At age 4½

Jennifer began to emphatically say that she had not grown in Gloria's womb. Over time, Jennifer's mom had explained her adoption story in simple terms, including that Jennifer had grown in Gloria's womb.

This "theory" of grief is contrary to the findings of David Brodzinsky, Ph.D., who has examined extensively how adopted children come to understand their adopted status. His findings are consistent with learning theory. Brodzinsky states that "sometime around 8 to 10 years of age, children begin to understand what relinquishment means. In middle childhood, reflection begins on the adoption process itself. This is a normal part of coping with adoption." Brodzinsky does not oppose early telling, but does caution parents to recognize that children do not understand the world in the same way adults do, and that any attempt at explaining must take this fact into account.

When one considers the example used by Silber and Dorner, one questions the accuracy of their interpretation of the child's response. Because it is unlikely that the child understands what adoption means and she has clearly denied the existence of her "birth mother," it is more likely that she is responding not to feelings of loss, but to confusion at her mother's insistence that she is not her mother. *Children of Open Adoption* is full of stories like Jennifer's, and one has to wonder what this constant reminder of differences will do to these children in the long run. What will happen when the children are old enough truly to understand adoption? Will they understand what their place is between two mothers?

Children Are at Greatest Risk

Marianne Berry, in an extensive literature review on open adoption, concludes:

Children, as children, are at greatest risk in open adoptions. Although openness and information sharing may prevent genealogical bewilderment and pain of outreach in adolescence, research findings so far have not found that openness leads to greater adjustment or attachment. Children do not understand the relationship in open adoption, and direct contact with a biological parent can weaken the bond between adoptive parents and child.

She states further:

> Without more information on the extent of open adoption practices and their long-term effects on all members of the adoption triad, practitioners must proceed with caution in prescribing openness, particularly when it includes direct contact between biological parents and children. When such openness is part of the adoptive triangle, adoption workers must be prepared to remain an integral part of the adoption triangle, providing postplacement support of all parties during the adoptee's growing up.

If the practice of open adoption does not improve the situation for the adopted person, the person who places the child, or the adoptive family, and in fact may increase the risks for each, it appears unwise to continue its practice. Studies of participants in adoption have shown that for the vast majority, traditional adoption has worked very well. For those who are continuing to have problems, it is first necessary to assess what is causing the problems and then to prescribe appropriate interventions to address and resolve those problems.

"The breadth and depth of satisfaction that participants [in open adoption] feel is impressive."

An Open Adoption Policy Is Best

James L. Gritter

James L. Gritter is a child welfare supervisor at Catholic Human Services in Michigan and author of several books on open adoption. In the following viewpoint, Gritter asserts that maintaining ongoing relationships between birth parents, adoptees, and adoptive parents after adoption can be the most beneficial arrangement. He claims that secrecy in adoption, although intended to protect birth parents and adoptees, has resulted in shame. Open adoption, according to Gritter, removes the secrecy and shame and promotes enduring relationships between those affected by adoption.

As you read, consider the following questions:
1. According to Gritter, how does closed adoption affect adoption workers?
2. In Gritter's opinion, how does secrecy function as a means of control in adoption?
3. What happens if adoption is not based on honor, according to the author?

Scenes and sensations from the days preceding open adoption are seared into my memory forever. In those days, it was routine for a birthparent to put her total trust in me, an act of phenomenal faith that terrified both of us. To find peace of mind and justify this massive trust, she told herself that this was a reasonable thing to do. She reasoned: "You're a nice person, and it's clear that you care about me and my baby. I think you might even be halfway on the ball. I know you'll put my baby with a wonderful, loving family, won't you? Won't you??" That logic may have relieved some of her anxiety, but it added significantly to mine. She needed more reassurance than I could realistically offer. I especially remember the unnerving comment of one birthmother who looked me in the eye and declared, "I don't worry about the adoptive parents at all because I'm sure they are just like you." In the absence of real information, I, of all people, represented the fantasy parents.

A Wrenching Undertaking

The moments of separation were especially daunting. I recall many occasions when I would peer into a hospital room to make sure I was in the right place. The young lady I had come to know and respect from weeks of planning would be there resting, her face radiating the contentment and fulfillment unique to a fresh mother. My arrival never failed to affect the atmosphere dramatically. In an instant, the tranquillity drained from her face, replaced by four-alarm panic. I was the social work equivalent of the Grim Reaper, on site to claim her baby. The necessary work accomplished, I would hustle back to the office to debrief with my kindred-spirit colleague, Abbie Nelson. Together we would commiserate, weep, and decide to resign from this wrenching undertaking. I knew I was not cut out for life as an adoption worker; I knew that, over time, this work would dull the parts of me I liked the best. There was only so much of the wilting pain of permanent separation that I could tolerate. A few weeks later, though, the withering drama would resume as I accompanied the wide-eyed birthmother to court, where the judge would ask whether it was her intention to "execute" a release of parental rights. Her rights would be "terminated," and her life as a ghost would begin. . . .

Unscouted Territory

Open adoption was not necessary just for the benefit of the birthparents, adoptive parents, and adoptees—it was also necessary for me.

When we shifted from closed to open adoption, we knew that all of us—birthparents, adoptive parents, adoptees, and professionals—were heading into a wilderness of unscouted possibilities where all things were possible. We probably should have been consumed with fear, but, oddly, we were not. Although there was no way at that point to predict the effectiveness of the open approach to adoption, we looked to the future with confidence. We were convinced that there had to be a better way. Our confidence was based on the simple belief that an approach based on candor and transparency would not lead to disaster. From a less positive perspective, we were sufficiently disenamored with the closed system to conclude that we did not have much to lose.

It was immediately clear to us that the open approach to adoption felt better. We were encouraged and excited, but the change to full open adoption did not occur overnight. We learned that clients ask for the amount of openness that we as workers were comfortable in offering. Since we had a substantial amount of consolidating and growing to do as professionals, client requests for open adoption started slowly and grew gradually. Looking back, I feel sad for those who failed to take advantage of the innovations available during our transition, but the gradual pace of change kept us from feeling overwhelmed. . . .

In the early days, every open adoption was a novel foray into exotic territory; and every adoption constituted an obvious opportunity to learn. Operating without the benefit of experience, we had no protocol; every decision required fresh thinking. Lacking precedent, we had no idea what was "normal" in open adoption and what was not. Happily, with the passage of time, the territory feels less exotic and less anxious. Our trepidation has been replaced with pleasant anticipation as we wonder what we will learn from each new arrangement that comes together.

The most crucial experience was surviving our first "catastrophe," otherwise known as a birthmother changing her mind about adoption after the prospective adoptive family had taken the baby into their home and hearts on an "at risk" basis. Because of our system's lingering overidentification with adoptive parents, we dreaded this possibility more than any other. There were many sins that could be overlooked in adoption, but we doubted that anyone could forgive the disappointing of a prospective adoptive family. They were, after all, victims of severe biological disappointment, card-carrying members of the middle class, paying customers, and most likely future board members. Lurking in the unconscious somewhere was the impression that it would be a simple matter for a disappointed couple to make a social worker's life miserable.

Our first "disaster" started in typically promising fashion. The birthmother selected the Thomases, a particularly likable family with a laid back lifestyle. The families were obviously compatible, and plans moved forward. The baby was born healthy and adorable. The prospective adoptive mother's mother flew from a distant state to lend an experienced hand to the awesome project of baby care. Shortly after arrival, grandma bought church raffle tickets in the names of each of her grandchildren. In story book fashion, the new baby was a hundred-dollar raffle winner; the omens were all positive.

A Dramatic Shift

Two weeks later, the scene shifted dramatically. The birthfather decided to pursue custody, a prospect that the birthmother found abhorrent. Panicked by that possibility, she decided to summarily resolve the matter by resuming custody of the baby herself. An unprecedented moment of truth was upon us.

We called the Thomases with the news and listened to their stunned silence over the phone. The plan called for them to return the baby the next day. We had failed our unofficial social work mandate to engineer a happily-ever-after outcome, and our fears had 24 hours to multiply exponentially as we awaited the devastation of "the worst that could happen."

The next day, the Thomases carried the flag of all would-be adoptive families with magnificence. Through their tears, they shared with absolute sincerity, "This is a beautiful baby. She is relaxed, easy to take care of, and completely lovable. What's more, she's a prizewinning baby, and we want to share this"—the envelope with the raffle winnings—"so everybody gets off to a good start. We are thankful for the opportunity to be part of her life story. God bless this new family."

A bitter family might have stalled our progress indefinitely, but the Thomases blessed our program with extraordinary grace and dignity under unimaginable pressure. They moved the program forward by demonstrating that we could survive the worst that could happen. They taught us that prospective adoptive parents are stronger and more loving than we had ever recognized in the days of our patronizing overprotection. And, as fate would have it, during the two weeks the Thomases had the baby, they conceived miraculously and truly did live happily ever after.

Hinging On Integrity

Over the years, our language for these situations has shifted from *catastrophe* to *disaster* to *reversal* to *turnabout* to *change of heart*. Michael Spry, one of the most insightful adoptive parents to go through our program, and an outspoken advocate for ethical standards in the field, noted that there is a certain justice in the change-of-heart circumstance. Prospective adoptive parents are asked to do what they have asked birthparents to consider; namely, placing a treasured child into someone else's arms. Just or unjust, these situations test the characters of everyone involved; and in an odd way, they constitute some of the most beautiful moments for our program. We marvel at the strength of character demonstrated by prospective parents in the face of devastated hope. Open adoption hinges on their integrity.

For all the risks associated with open adoption, it was quickly apparent that our adoptive parents enjoyed it. They liked the candor. They liked the greater control over the experience that open adoption gave them. They liked the improved information they received. They liked the chance to be involved with the baby in the hospital. They liked being able to express gratitude to the people who deserved it. They just plain liked it. . . .

Secrecy and Shame

The adoption scene was dominated for decades by secrecy. For years, I understood secrecy from three perspectives: historic, functional, and problematic. From the vantage point of history, clearly secrecy was well intended. It developed as a means to protect adoptees and birthparents from the censure of their communities. The goal of secrecy was to spare them the stigma of devastating labels like "bastard" and "fallen woman" at a time in history when such diminished status was disastrous. In positive terms, secrecy sought to preserve the opportunity for adoptees and birthparents to participate in their communities as full-status members. It is crucial to note, however, that the protection offered birthparents and adoptees was from the censure of the community not from each other.

The historical perspective is useful to explain the origin of secrecy; but in the face of dramatically altered social conditions, it does not explain its continuation. With the stigma of illegitimacy fading rapidly, the need for protection has dwindled. What, then, sustains the secret-based system? If it does not meet the needs of most adoptees and birthparents, why keep it? The obvious answer is that it meets someone else's needs. Two major groups have lobbied for the retention of secrecy: adoptive parents and adoption professionals. Many adoptive parents fear openness because they are afraid they will somehow lose their children. Secrecy gives them the power of exclusivity, but sadly, power is an unpromising foundation for enduring family life. Secrecy also made adoption practitioners powerful. As the only fully informed players in the drama, adoption workers were in total control of the process. Their control was cemented by the privilege of confidentiality, which insulated them from any form of accountability. I am convinced, to the extent it perseveres, the current function of secrecy is more control than protection.

Most of the time, I simply viewed secrecy as a problem. It was the enemy and, as such, was a factor to contend with and overcome. A disheartening amount of my time was and is spent attending to the aftermath of secrecy as searching birthparents and adoptees ask assistance in their search efforts. Let there be no confusion about this: Secrecy is a tremendous problem for adoptees. The institution claims that, more than anything, it seeks to serve the adoptee; but judging by performance, the institution has obviously lied.

Diminishing Grief

Counselors to birthmothers have postulated that these women experience extended loss and grief following the placement of children for adoption. Open adoption gives biological parents more control over the adoption decision by providing information about the adoptive parents who will be receiving their child. Having this information enables the birthparents to imagine or visualize the family environment in which their child will live and may relieve some of the guilt and uncertainty that accompany relinquishing a child. The counseling process throughout the preparations for open adoption is thought to facilitate the biological parents' grieving and their decision making about the adoption itself.

Marianne Berry, *Future of Children*, Spring 1993.

More recently, I have come to understand secrecy from a fourth perspective: as a symptom. Secrecy is symptomatic of a much deeper issue—namely, shame. Adoption founders as an institution because it is built on a foundation of shame. For decades, adoption has functioned essentially as a two-step process of disowning and owning. In that form, it is an almost perfect script for shame, for there is great shame in disowning and owning; and, obviously, there is great shame in being disowned and in being owned. Shame is a matter of defect, powerlessness, and rejection—all familiar themes in adoption. Very familiar. . . .

Sometimes people interested in adoption are pigeonholed into one of two camps. There are those who are for adoption, and those who are against it. I find that a pitiful simplification of the issues. Adoption is not a singular phenomena. Am I in favor of a shame-perpetuating form of adoption? Absolutely not. Am I in favor of an honor-based approach to adoption? Certainly. An honoring form of adoption will never eliminate the pain, but it can without question generate beauty. I have seen situations where adoption returned the sparkle of life to the eyes of everyone involved. When a 3-month-old child's eyes change from vacant to inquisitive in two day's time, something undeniably important is going on. . . .

The Need for Honor

The shame that has dominated adoption for so many years must be replaced with honor. Yes, honor. Some will no doubt scoff at this idea. They live in a mercenary world of calculation and expediency and have concluded that honor is an archaic, perhaps even silly, idea. They have given up on honor. They operate in a value-drained world where cynicism prevails. Instead of making a case against honor, I believe they document the need for it.

We need honor, but it frightens us because it calls us to personal responsibility. All of us long for honor, and each of us, as a private act of moral courage, is fully capable of producing it. Furthermore, if anything can motivate us to seek honor, I believe it is the innocence of children. If we cannot hazard the vulnerability of honor for the sake of children, the cynicism is deserved. . . .

Honor—profound respect for others—is crucial to the institution of adoption. Without it, adoption quickly degenerates into exploitation.

Can honor truly function as the foundation for adoption? The field's foremost expert, Sharon Kaplan-Roszia, wisely describes the experience of open adoption as "life." Given that insight, the question becomes, how will life play in this arena, which, because it is premised on upward psychological mobility, is somehow supposed to be better than life? A local reporter put the issue in sharp focus with an insightful question. "Would you, if you could," he asked, choosing his words carefully, "undo the openness of any of the adoptions you have arranged?" That one made me think. Certainly not all of our adoptions have been wonderful. Some people were admitted to our program who should have been screened out. Some initially promising participants ultimately proved disappointing. If we could, we would surely change some players, but would we change the openness? The answer, after careful deliberation, is a firm "No." To my knowledge, after watching more than 400 open adoptions come together through our program, the privileges of openness have been handled responsibly. We would not undo the openness of any of them.

The Spirit of Hope

Open adoption really does work—not every time and not with equally satisfying results each time—but it does work. The breadth and depth of satisfaction that participants feel is impressive. When open adoption is based on genuine candor, unpressured choice, and enduring respect, it reliably produces remarkable results. When we first tried this style of adoption, there was no way we could know the creative forms it would take. Now, with the benefit of extensive experience, we are better informed. Our conclusion? The variety and depth of the open adoption relationships that our families enjoy surpass anything we imagined in our most optimistic moments. . . .

The nurturing culture of a healthy open adoption system brings out the honor in people. This is most clear in moments when plans change. We have witnessed tremendous courage, grace, and dignity under wilting pressure. We have seen friendships persevere even when there was no placement. We have observed reversals of fortune and role in which birthparents have ministered to adoptive parents going through difficulties. . . .

Although the basic "Can it work?" question is settled, it is not time to relax. The freedom of open adoption permits—perhaps even invites—distortion and excess. As open adoptions become more common, exotic and unpleasant cases will surely arise. These unfortunate situations will not disprove the potential of open adoption. They will remind us that there are many variations on the theme and that they are not equally promising. . . .

If we can overcome our fears and trust our better instincts, we can replace the debilitation of shame with the promise of honor. As we grow in our ability to honor each other, we breathe new life into a weary institution. As we sincerely honor children, we kindle the amazing, affirming spirit of open adoption.

> "The question is whether adoptees' birth
> mothers ought to be stripped of their
> confidentiality even though they were
> promised they wouldn't be."

Adoption Records Should Remain Sealed

Ira Carnahan

In American adoption, birth records have traditionally been
sealed to protect birth parents and children from the stigma of
adoption and unwed parenthood. Today, many birth parents
establish relationships with their children after adoption while
others wish to remain anonymous. In the following viewpoint,
Ira Carnahan contends that adoption records should remain
sealed if the birth parent requests it. Carnahan contends the
movement to make sealed adoption records accessible to all
adult adoptees, spearheaded by the adoptee rights organization Bastard Nation, threatens the right to confidentiality in
adoption. He adds that vital medical and background information is already disclosed to adoptees; therefore, only birth
parents should be allowed to release identifying information.
Carnahan is a freelance writer in Washington, D.C.

As you read, consider the following questions:
1. According to Carnahan, how does Bastard Nation
   advance its agenda?
2. How does the author respond to the claim that many
   birth mothers want to be contacted by the children they
   placed for adoption?
3. How does Carnahan support his opinion that ending
   confidentiality in adoptions may increase the rate of
   abortion?

When Jane Doe No. 1 decided to place her baby for adoption in 1961, she was promised her decision would be kept confidential. That's what the law said in Oregon, where her baby was born, and that's what her doctor, a nun, and the attorney handling the adoption assured her, too. Jane, 21 and unmarried, gave up her baby and went on with her life. By 1998 she had a husband and four kids, none of whom knew about her other child.

That soon threatened to change. An Oregon adoptee named Helen Hill, working with an activist group called Bastard Nation, launched a campaign to throw out the state's laws shielding the names of mothers who place children for adoption. Such laws aren't fair to adoptees, they argued. "You can't cut a human being off from knowledge of their roots," Hill said. "It's a really inhumane thing to do."

Disclosure of Confidential Information

Hill and Bastard Nation campaigned hard for the "open records" initiative. Oregon voters responded, approving it in November 1998 with fifty-seven percent of the vote. Shortly after, Jane and several other anonymous birth mothers filed suit. "Having kept this secret from my family and community these many years, disclosure of confidential information would be worse for me now than it would have been at the time that the events occurred," Jane wrote in an affidavit.

"The events surrounding the child's birth and my decision to place her for adoption in 1961 were among the most difficult and emotionally painful I have ever experienced," she explained. "If that confidential information is released, I will have absolutely no control over its use and publication to other persons, including my husband and children."

Too bad, the courts declared. In a string of rulings, which the U.S. Supreme Court recently let stand, judges held that the promises made to mothers giving up babies weren't legally binding and that the mothers have no right to privacy. And so the Oregon Health Division is now mailing out thousands of formerly sealed birth certificates.

Encouraged by its success in Oregon, Bastard Nation is looking to change the law in other states. In Alabama, the governor recently signed an open-records bill modeled on

Oregon's, and in Tennessee, an open-records law recently went into effect. In Delaware, a law opening birth certificates with some limits took effect in 1999. And in Washington state, Bastard Nation and other activists are gearing up for an open-records initiative in 2001 like the one in Oregon.

No Belief in Compromise

Founded in 1996, Bastard Nation doesn't believe in compromise. It opposes laws already on the books in most states that promote contact between birth mother and child when both want it, but that give birth mothers the option to withhold release of their names and other identifying information. Such laws are unacceptable, declares a group publication called the *Basic Bastard:* "Any legislation that provides for less than access on demand, without compromise, is a violation of the basic right to equal protection under the law as guaranteed by the Fourteenth Amendment to the U.S. Constitution."

To advance its agenda, the group publishes the *Bastard Quarterly*, which provides "a forum for Bastard Nationals to express themselves." An essay by one of the group's founders proclaims: "In Bastard Nation, adoptees have found a voice. We are loud, powerful and ready to demand justice in the form of open records. The Era of the Bastard has arrived."

Bastard Nation's rhetoric and tactics resemble those of gay activist groups such as Queer Nation and ACT UP. Take the protest the group held in 1999 in front of the D.C. headquarters of the National Council for Adoption, whose founding president, William Pierce, is the leading defender of the confidentiality of records: "Clad in black T-shirts emblazoned with a bright gold logo called a 'spermburst,' the Bastard Nation protesters chant, 'Willie P, Willie P, why are you afraid of me?'" the *Washington City Paper* reported. "On Bastard Nation political buttons, his exaggeratedly scraggly face is depicted with a diagonal rubout line across it. He was hung in effigy at a previous rally. . . . 'We shall put this beast in chains and shall vanquish him utterly,' roars Marley Greiner, the self-described 'founding foundling' of Bastard Nation."

Greiner, the executive chair of Bastard Nation, refers to mothers as "breeders," spells America with a "k," and signs her postings to Internet chat rooms "by all means necessary." Yet she blames the ugliness of the adoption records debate squarely on the other side. "I personally think that Bill Pierce has made civil discourse on adoption almost impossible in this country today," she says.

Clever Propaganda

Pierce, an avuncular 64-year-old former executive at the Child Welfare League of America, begs to differ. "What you're dealing with are very, very clever propagandists," he says. "They are quite skillful." That skill comes through on Bastard Nation's website (*www.bastards.org*) and in the way the group seeks to frame the adoption records debate. It's not about balancing birth mothers' and adoptees' interests, or assessing the effect of opening records on the number of adoptions. No, it's a simple matter of civil rights.

"We feel that humans have a fundamental right to their identity, and that the government should not be putting up impediments to keep people from accessing their own vital records," says Ron Morgan, who lives in San Francisco and is one of three members of Bastard Nation's executive committee. "We feel that it's a civil right for us to access them."

Bastard Nation members also talk a lot about their pride and dignity. The group's mission statement declares, "We have reclaimed the badge of bastardy placed on us by those who would attempt to shame us; we see nothing shameful in having been born out of wedlock or in being adopted." But this defiant stance seems a bit odd. No one today, after all, suggests that adoptees should feel any shame. The question is whether adoptees' birth mothers ought to be stripped of their confidentiality even though they were promised they wouldn't be.

Improve the System of Release

In arguing they should be, adoptee-rights activists make a number of dubious claims. One is that adoptees need the names of their birth parents so that they can obtain vital medical background information. This claim appeals to the public. The truth, though, is that Oregon and other states already provide for the release of medical information when needed, without disclosing the mother's identity if she wishes to remain anonymous. To be sure, the release of information often isn't as easy or complete as it could be. But the obvious solution is to improve the system of release; there's no need to compromise birth mothers' confidentiality.

Another claim, often repeated by journalists, is that nearly all birth mothers want to be contacted, so not opening birth records is denying the wishes of the many to satisfy the desires of a reclusive few. But that appears untrue. While the precise percentage isn't clear, Pierce suggests at least one-third of birth mothers don't want personal contact, as revealed by their responses when contacted by state-authorized intermediaries in Oregon, prior to the new law, and in Florida.

Adoption Confidentiality and Rates of Abortion

The most controversial claim of adoptee-rights activists is that abolishing confidentiality won't lead more women to seek abortions. Pierce says that's absurd. "It's a no-brainer," he says. "Put yourself in the position of a young woman. All you have to do is look at countries where they do not allow, in essence, any privacy for adoption and they allow privacy for abortion, like Japan, and you find almost no adoptions and you find abortions are almost universally the option of choice. Because a choice which is not private is no choice at all."

That's not just Pierce's view. Jeremiah Gutman, former chairman of the American Civil Liberties Union's privacy committee, has written that a pregnant woman "may be inclined to bring the pregnancy to term rather than secure an abortion, but, if she cannot rely upon the adoption agency or attorney and the law to protect her privacy, and to conceal her identity for all time, her choice to go the abortion route may be compelled by that lack of confidence in confidentiality."

Nonsense, replies Bastard Nation. As evidence that ending confidentiality won't lead to more abortions, the group cites below-average rates of abortion in Kansas and Alaska, which have long had open birth records. But the fact that abortion rates are below the national average in these two states is not a surprise, given their demographics. If, instead, we compare the abortion rate in Kansas with the rates in nearby states where the demographics are similar, we find that Kansas's rate is well above average. Such statistical points aside, it is striking that Bastard Nation and other adoptee-rights groups, whose ranks are filled with ardent defenders of abortion, have no patience with a privacy argument on behalf of women who place babies for adoption.

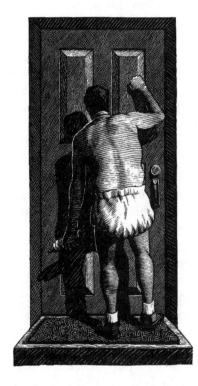

Patrick Arrasmith, *Weekly Standard*, September 11, 2000.

Why? Because it would limit adoptees' rights. And that won't do. "The underlying principle of the adoption movement is the determination to be free of those limitations that have not been imposed on non-adopted citizens," declares an article on Bastard Nation's website. "The issue is whether adoptees are to be allowed to emancipate from chattel-child status into autonomous adults, or are they to continue to be infantilized by the ongoing control of the State and agency, birth parents and adoptive parents?"

Blood, Biology, and Identity

Not all adoptees who seek open records are so militant. While those who are politicized talk about their rights, the unpoliticized talk about their wounds. One man wrote recently in the *Oregonian*, the state's largest newspaper, "As an adoptee, I have been drifting, lost, most of my life." He was, he said, "driven unconsciously to solve the riddle of my blood."

This notion of blood and biology as central to identity runs deep in adoptee-rights rhetoric. "One's biological history is as much a part of the essential self as limbs or senses," argues an article on the Bastard Nation site. "To be deprived of knowledge of one's origins and ancestry is to be maimed as surely as to be deprived of limbs or sight." It is one of the oddities of the adoption records debate that the typically left-leaning advocates of open records stress the importance of genes and blood, while advocates of sealed records, who are often on the right, have little use for such talk.

While Bastard Nation's main interest lies in opening adoption records, the group is also moving into other areas. The most prominent is opposition to so-called safe haven laws, which allow mothers who would otherwise abandon newborns in dumpsters or alleys instead to drop them off, no questions asked, at designated centers, where the children can then be placed for adoption. Such laws are sweeping through state legislatures, and Bastard Nation is appalled. While the group raises several objections, the one that most obviously explains its interest in the issue is its claim that safe haven laws "obliterate the identity rights of the abandoned child." The group condemns the laws—intended to prevent infant deaths—for "lifting entirely the obligation to collect and record any identity information, in contravention of the widely recognized human right to an identity."

The Unintended Effect

While Bastard Nation likely won't have much success with this argument, the prospects for open adoption records look brighter. In fact, with the rise of "open adoption," in which birth parents, adoptive parents, and adoptees keep in contact, the number of birth parents requiring confidentiality is falling. E. Wayne Carp, a historian of adoption at Pacific

Lutheran University in Tacoma, Washington, suggests too that opening records probably won't sharply reduce the number of children placed for adoption since the number of children put up for adoption in the United States is already low. "I would say if we look out at the adoption picture now it could hardly get fewer," he says. "The numbers have been shrinking without open records as it is. It's a remarkable figure that almost 98 percent of women who give birth to children out of wedlock keep them now," he says. "It's unbelievable, but they do."

Even if the further weakening of adoption isn't Bastard Nation's goal—and they say it isn't—this might be an unintended effect. Pierce, of the National Council for Adoption, points abroad as a warning of what could happen here. In 1975, England and Wales moved from confidential records to open records. Since then the annual number of adoptions of children under age one has plummeted from 4,548 to just 322 in 1995, a 93 percent decline. "The data are clear and unequivocal," Pierce says. "Infant adoption is a relic in England and Wales."

Could the same thing happen here? It's hard to say. In England and Wales, the number of adoptions was already falling when records were unsealed. It's clear too that the number of adoptions is shaped by many factors, of which the law is just one. Yet it's hardly farfetched that ending confidentiality could lead fewer women to place babies for adoption. Within the next few years, we are likely to find out.

> *"Adoption should never ask any human being to trade their . . . right to know the true facts of one's own birth in return for a promise of a stable and loving home."*

Adoption Records Should Be Opened

Denise K. Castellucci

In the following viewpoint, Denise K. Castellucci argues that adoption records should be opened because only the adopted individual has the right to investigate or bypass the facts of his or her origins. As an adopted adult, Castellucci believes that withholding adoption records undermines the adopted adult's right to his or her heritage and identity. For instance, she claims that sealed record laws have prevented some adults from obtaining passports. Castellucci is national coordinator of National Adoptee Rights Day and founder of Voices of Adoption, an Internet-based adoption resource center.

As you read, consider the following questions:
1. How does Castellucci illustrate her claim that a birth is in part a public event?
2. According to the author, what was the original purpose of sealing adoption records?
3. How does Castellucci respond to the argument that birth mothers oppose open record laws?

Reprinted, with permission, from "Privacy, Confidentiality, and Anonymity in Adoption," by Denise K. Castellucci, June 5, 2000, web article found at www.ibar.com/voices/opinion/dkc/privacy.html.

The recent adoptee rights victories in Alabama and Oregon have renewed the debate over the merits and risks of open records. The mainstream media incorrectly frames the debate as birthmothers' privacy versus the adoptees' right to know. It is truly a debate between those who would benefit by the return to shame and secrecy in adoption versus those who think that adoption would benefit by more truth, transparency, and accountability. The opponents of open records fear that if adult adoptees and birthfamilies have access to the truth in what really happened that they may have some explaining to do. Rather than being up front about their motives, they confuse an individual's desire to remain anonymous from their offspring and pasts with the right of privacy. Fortunately, the courts have consistently been able to see through these arguments.

As a supporter of adoptee rights and open records laws, I have often been asked, "Do people have a fundamental right to know who gave birth to them? If my mother does not want me to know who she is, do I have a right to invade her privacy and know who she is?"

A Private and Public Event

The courts have established that a birth is a private and public event and the state has long recorded births for a myriad of reasons. When there is a birth, it is recorded by the state and held for the person whose birth it records. It is important to note that birth records are not sealed upon relinquishment of a child to adoption, but sealed by the court as part of the finalization of an adoption. Children who are not adopted do not have their records sealed.

In order to understand this issue clearly, you need to be clear on the differences between the right to privacy, the need for confidentiality, and the desire for anonymity.

There are those who would say accessing your birth records is not in the U.S. Constitution, but neither is the right to privacy.

The Most Misunderstood Concept

The right to privacy is perhaps the most misunderstood concept because it is not specifically mentioned in the Constitution, and needs to be fleshed out by the courts. The right to privacy primarily concerns itself with the relationship between the state and the individual. For instance, prior to the 1965 *Griswald v. Connecticut* Supreme Court decision, possessing birth control was illegal in the state of Connecticut. The Griswald decision established a zone of privacy when it came to family planning and one's bedroom. It held that the state could not pass a law which essentially pulls government into the bedrooms of individuals. The *Roe v. Wade* decision further established that the state cannot make reproductive choices for women in regards to whether they carry a child to term or terminate a pregnancy. That case created a zone of privacy in a woman's womb. It is important to note that opponents to open records used these cases and other cases involving the right to privacy in their challenge of the access law in Tennessee, but the courts found that they were not able to establish a zone of privacy for birthmothers.

There have also been cases that limit the right to privacy, which clearly establishes that the right to privacy is not absolute. Despite their rhetoric, the opponents to open records were not asking for the right to privacy, but the ability for a woman to be forever anonymous from her offspring. Courts found that the right to be forever anonymous from one's own offspring did not exist, and allowing adult adoptees to access their own birth records does not violate the right to privacy.

The Need for Confidentiality

Then there is the need for confidentiality. Whenever we seek services from health professionals or any other services, there is a professional courtesy and obligation to extend confidential services, which doesn't mean to keep information away from those the services affect, but keep information from outsiders. The original intent of adoption records laws was not to protect parties from each other, but to protect the parties from public scrutiny and discrimination. Laws passed in Oregon and in Alabama only issue the original birth certificate to the adoptee whose birth it records from the office of vital records (not the agency), and those do not make the document public. Since these laws do not make these government records public record, they do not violate confidentiality agreements made by agencies. Our laws provide exceptions that do not make confidentiality absolute. For instance, as a confidential counselor to abused women, I was compelled by the state to betray the confidence and report to the authorities if her children's welfare was at stake. E-mail and correspondence that was once assumed to be confidential can be inspected by employers for any reason.

Overwhelmingly in Favor

Parents of adopted children in New York are overwhelmingly in favor of laws that allow adult adoptees access to information in their birth certificates about their birth parents, according to a Cornell study.

"One major argument for keeping records sealed is to protect adoptive parents who might feel threatened if their adopted children knew more about their birth parents," says Rosemary Avery, associate professor of consumer economics and housing and a specialist in family policy and foster care.

"Yet, these results indicate there is no justification for keeping such information from adult adoptees, especially non-identifying information," Avery says. "And there is no reason to believe that New York State adoptive parents are any different from those in other states: they are overwhelmingly supportive of opening sealed adoption records."

Susan S. Lang, *Human Ecology Forum*, Spring 1997.

Then there is a desire to be anonymous from one's own offspring and events from one's own past. As imperfect human beings, we all have had times we would like to block out and wish not be reminded of. That wish is very compelling indeed. There is always a freedom to take steps to make oneself anonymous from someone and make events from our pasts unknown, but we cannot look to government to protect ourselves from our own pasts; to do so would embroil government into our own personal business. Sealed records do not guarantee that a birthmother's wish to divorce herself from her past will be absolute. Countless search and reunions happen everyday in sealed records states. Sealed records laws actually give a false sense of security to these women, by offering guarantees that are not enforceable.

The plain truth is that we are all the product of all events in our lives regardless of how difficult they are to face. A birthmother is always going to be a biological mother to a human being with shared ancestry and medical history, no matter how much she may wish it not be so or how many barriers the state imposes. The courts in Oregon and in Tennessee were not blind to the desire for some birthmothers to not revisit the "unblessed event," but found that government could not violate basic rights of adopted adults in order to pacify them.

The Interests of Adopted Adults

In the balance of interests, the courts have found that the interests of adopted adults were more compelling and that open records laws do not violate U.S. or state constitutions.

The plain fact is that laws passed by Oregon and Alabama do not infringe on the right of a birthmother to regulate who enters her life. There is no right to a relationship with anyone, and as adults we should have the ability to free association and regulate our own interpersonal relationships.

All states that seal records have always allowed adoptees to petition the courts to open their adoption records for "good cause" without the court notifying birthparents. For the past 20 years there has been a search and reunion movement that has been well documented in the press. In view of these facts, it is absurd to think there has been an unquestionable expectation that one would not be found by one's offspring or one's birthparent.

No Support for Promises

In Oregon, opponents of Measure 58 argued that the law violated promises of lifelong anonymity of birthmothers from their offspring. The courts took a close look at the legislative history of adoption statutes in Oregon and found that there was nothing to support such promises in the law and that those who made such promises were not authorized agents of the state. The fact that the state regulated how adoptions were to be handled did not make those who practiced adoptions agents of the state. The legislature and the voters could not be held hostage to those who may have misinterpreted or wished to rewrite adoption statutes. The fact is that these individuals made various promises, from telling women they will be able to meet their child when they turn 18 to promises of lifelong anonymity, but the statutes did not support any of these promises. If a realtor promised in the 1950s to a potential homeowner that the neighborhood and local school will always be white only, one could not be granted immunity from civil rights laws that make that illegal. While the realtor is regulated by the state, his/her promises cannot bind legislators or the voters forever to those promises.

I think it is unreasonable to ask any human being to divorce themselves from the facts of their own birth, and to expect that adopted citizens should endure more scrutiny and regulation than any other citizens based only on the circumstances of their births. Interest or disinterest in one's own origins should be a personal decision of the individual, not a decision made by government or any other other individual. I know many adoptees who have been unable to get passports due to the fact that they are unable to establish the true facts of their births.

As a reunited adult adoptee, I can now trace my roots to the 1300s. Yet, when I stand in line at my local vital statistics office with other adult citizens with the names of several generations of my birthfamily, I get only a blank piece of paper. The only thing that separates me from others who stand in line is the circumstances of my birth. Based on the circumstances of my birth, state laws place me in a suspect class of citizens in fear of what *might* happen if I were able to gain the true facts of my birth.

The Most Basic Right

Opponents to open records like to present hypothetical situations and what-ifs as having more weight than rights and dignity of adult adoptees, not out of any true concern for those touched by adoption, but in fear of being held accountable for the false promises made or having light shown on their practices. If these laws were so caustic to birthmothers as opponents claim, why is it there is no birthparent group that opposes such laws? You would think that if even one birthmother would be hurt under open records there would be opposition by groups who would be most qualified to be intimately familiar with what these women went through.

Adoption should never ask any human being to trade their dignity, self-determination, and the most basic right to know the true facts of one's own birth in return for a promise of a stable and loving home. When you deny rights and dignity to adoptees you do the same to their children, grandchildren, and generations after. How their interests can be trumped by someone who fears her life will become messy is the most absurd notion of all.

| *"Eliminating family preservation and amending 'reasonable efforts' [requirements to preserve biological ties] guarantees the needless destruction of . . . loving families."*

Policies Should Emphasize Family Preservation

National Coalition for Child Protection Reform

The National Coalition for Child Protection Reform (NCCPR) is an organization that promotes family preservation and child welfare reform. In the following viewpoint, the NCCPR argues that policies designed to protect child safety by restricting family preservation efforts actually harm children. It claims that many children are removed from their homes for "neglect" when in fact their parents are simply poor. Therefore, the NCCPR asserts that programs that support family preservation and counter the effects of economic hardship are better suited to serve the needs of disadvantaged children.

As you read, consider the following questions:
1. In the NCCPR's opinion, how does the definition of "neglect" harm an impoverished family?
2. How does the NCCPR support their claim that family preservation programs work?
3. According to the author, how is adoption problematic?

Excerpted from *Issue Papers on Family Preservation, Foster Care, and "Reasonable Efforts,"* published by the National Coalition for Child Protection Reform (NCCPR) at www.nccpr.org/newissues/index.html. Reprinted with permission.

A child dies at the hand of a parent.
Within days, sometimes hours, it becomes known that this child was "known to the system."

For most people, such a case is their introduction to the child welfare system. And naturally, they have one overriding question—how could it have happened?

Lately, politicians and self-proclaimed "child advocates" have been suggesting an answer that is simple, easy—and wrong.

They blame "family preservation." Or they blame a federal law that required states and localities to make "reasonable efforts" to keep families together. Or they blame both.

It is claimed that "family preservation" is at odds with "child protection." It is claimed that family preservation must be eliminated and the "reasonable efforts" clause repealed or amended in order to protect children. It was even claimed that the "reasonable efforts" clause causes children to languish in foster care. In fact, "reasonable efforts" is all that prevents the foster care crisis from being even worse.

The Campaign Against Family Preservation

And now it is getting worse. The smear campaign against family preservation was successful. In 1997, Congress passed legislation that effectively repeals the "reasonable efforts" requirement in federal law. As a result, even as so many other social indicators are improving—crime is down, unemployment is down, even child abuse itself is down—the foster care population is still going up. The only hope for thousands of children rests with how states and localities choose to use the new power the federal government has given them. By and large, they have not used it well.

The demands to abolish family preservation and "reasonable efforts" come with some great applause lines. Such demands are said to involve "erring on the side of the child" or "defending children's rights" or "putting children first." But abolishing family preservation does nothing of the kind.

Rather, this approach requires the massive removal of children from one set of adults—their parents—to another set of adults, foster parents or orphanage workers, with the decisions made by still another set of adults, judges, lawyers and, especially, workers for government and private child welfare agencies. In the 19th Century such workers proudly called themselves "child savers." Abolishing family preservation puts child savers, not children, first. And when "child savers" come first, children come last.

"Putting children first" is a euphemism for taking more and more children away from their parents and placing them in foster care. But contrary to stereotype, family preservation is safer than foster care.

Those who oppose family preservation say they want to remove children from danger to safety. Often, it turns out to be the other way around.

The attempt to scapegoat "family preservation" has had disastrous consequences for children. Indeed, in some cities, the consequences have been fatal.

Critics claim that family preservation "dominates" the system. But the number of children in foster care has increased from 270,000 in 1985 to at least 568,000 today. If those of us who advocate family preservation have been so "dominant," what are all those children doing in foster care?

Critics claim children languish in foster care because of the "reasonable efforts" requirement. But relative to the total child population, there were at least as many children in foster care before "reasonable efforts" became law in 1980. Bad as things were before 1997, with the effective repeal of "reasonable efforts," they are getting worse.

Eliminating family preservation and amending "reasonable efforts" guarantees the needless destruction of still more loving families, an even greater surge in the foster care population, and, worst of all, the senseless deaths of more children. . . .

The Myth of Classlessness

It is an article of faith among "child savers" that "child abuse crosses class lines." They tell us that we are as likely to find maltreatment in rich families as in poor, but the rich can hide from authorities. But like most child saver "truisms," this one is false. Prof. Leroy Pelton, chair of the Children and Family Services Concentration at the Salem State College School of Social Work calls it "The Myth of Classlessness."

Like the tailors in the fable of *The Emperor's New Clothes*, the child savers have invented a whole group of invisible, middle-class child abusers only they are wise enough to see. Of course there are some middle-class child abusers. But the evidence is overwhelming that poverty is by far the most important cause of child maltreatment—and the most important reason families end up in "the system" whether they have maltreated their children or not.

The federal government's *Third National Incidence Study of Child Abuse and Neglect* compared families with an annual income of under $15,000 to families with an annual income over $30,000. Their findings:

- Abuse is 14 times more common in poor families.
- Neglect is 44 times more common in poor families.

The study emphasized that the findings "cannot be plausibly explained on the basis of the higher visibility of lower income families to community professionals."

Studies in which all the subjects are equally open to public scrutiny (groups made up entirely of welfare recipients, for example) show that those who abuse tend to be the "poorest of the poor."

Three Reasons for Caution

The Adoption 2002 initiative and the related legislation sought to make adoption easier and to get children adopted at younger ages so they are not damaged by further maltreatment or by long waits in the child welfare system. These are important aims. Three reasons for caution, however, are (1) that systemic factors, such as poverty and single female parenthood, are ignored; (2) that poor and single-parent families may be disadvantaged, whereas people desiring to adopt may be advantaged; and (3) that the comparative effects of terminating parental rights on children and their biological families are not addressed.

Leslie Doty Hollingsworth, *Social Work*, March 2000.

The Myth of Classlessness doesn't just run counter to research. It runs counter to common sense. It is well-known that child abuse is linked to stress. It is equally well-known that poor families tend to be under more stress than rich families.

The gap between rich and poor is widest in the area of "neglect"—which makes up by far the largest single category of maltreatment reports. That's because the poor are included in our neglect laws almost by definition.

What is neglect? In Ohio, it's when a child's "condition or environment is such as to warrant the state, in the interests of the child, in assuming his guardianship." In Illinois, it's failure to provide "the proper or necessary support . . . for a child's well-being." In Mississippi, it's when a child is "without proper care, custody, supervision, or support." In South Dakota, it's when a child's "environment is injurious to his welfare."

Such definitions make a mockery of the oft-repeated child-saver claim that "we never remove children because of poverty alone."

Cases of "Neglect"

Imagine that you are an impoverished single mother with an eight-year-old daughter and a four-year-old son. The four-year-old is ill with a fever and you need to get him medicine. But you have no car, it's very cold, pouring rain, and it will take at least an hour to get to and from the pharmacy. You don't know most of your neighbors and those you know you have good reason not to trust. What do you do?

Go without the medicine? That's "medical neglect." The child savers can take away your children for medical neglect. Bundle up the feverish four-year-old in the only threadbare coat he's got and take him out in the cold and rain? That's "physical neglect." The child savers can take away your children for physical neglect. Leave the eight-year-old to care for the four-year-old and try desperately to get back home as soon as you can? That's "lack of supervision." The child savers can take away your children for lack of supervision.

And in every one of those cases, the child savers would say, with a straight face, that they didn't take your children "because of poverty alone."

Or consider some actual cases from around the country.

- In Orange County, California, an impoverished single mother can't find someone to watch her children while she works at night, tending a ride at a theme park. So she leaves her eight-, six-, and four-year-old children alone in the motel room that is the only housing they can afford. Someone calls child protective services. Instead of helping her with babysitting or daycare, they take away the children on the spot.

- In Akron, Ohio, a grandmother raises her 11-year-old granddaughter despite being confined to a wheelchair with a lung disease. Federal budget cuts cause her to lose housekeeping help. The house becomes filthy. Instead of helping with the housekeeping, child protective services takes the granddaughter away and throws her in foster care for a month. The child still talks about how lonely and terrified she was—and about the time her foster parent took her picture and put it in a photo album under the heading: "filthy conditions."
- In Los Angeles, the pipes in a grandmother's rented house burst, flooding the basement and making the home a health hazard. Instead of helping the family find another place to live, child protective workers take away the granddaughter and place her in foster care. She dies there, allegedly killed by her foster mother. The child welfare agency that would spend nothing to move the family offers $5,000 for the funeral. . . .

Even when child savers don't remove the children, the "help" they offer impoverished families can be a hindrance. For such families, demanding that they drop everything to go to a counselor's office or attend a parent education class is simply adding one more burden for people who already are overwhelmed.

Step one to ensuring they can provide a safe environment for their children is offering help to ameliorate the worst effects of poverty. Family preservation programs do just that. And that is one reason they succeed where other efforts fail. . . .

Family Preservation Works

Family preservation is one of the most intensively scrutinized programs in all of child welfare. Several studies—and real world experience—show that family preservation programs that follow the Homebuilders model safely prevent placement in foster care. [The Homebuilders program is a series of policies and procedures designed to intervene in family crises and encourage family preservation.]

Michigan's Families First program sticks rigorously to the

Homebuilders model. The Michigan program was evaluated by comparing children who received family preservation services to a "control group" that did not. After one year, among children who were referred because of abuse or neglect, the control group children were nearly twice as likely to be placed in foster care as the Families First children. Thirty-six percent of children in the control group were placed, compared to only 19.4 percent of the Families First children.

Another Michigan study went further. In this study, judges actually gave permission to researchers to "take back" some children they had just ordered into foster care and place them in Families First instead. One year later, 93 percent of these children still were in their own homes. And Michigan's State Auditor concluded that the Families First program "has generally been effective in providing a safe alternative to the out-of-home placement of children who are at imminent risk of being removed from the home. The program places a high priority on the safety of children."

An experiment in Utah and Washington State also used a comparison group. After one year, 85.2 percent of the children in the comparison group were placed in foster care, compared to only 44.4 percent of the children who received intensive family preservation services.

A study in California found that 55 percent of the control group children were placed, compared to only 26 percent of the children who received intensive family preservation services.

A North Carolina study comparing 1,254 families receiving Intensive Family Preservation Services (IFPS) to more than 100,000 families who didn't found that "IFPS consistently resulted in fewer placements.". . .

Ignoring the Evidence

Critics ignore all of this evidence preferring to repeatedly cite one study from Illinois which found that that state's family preservation programs were ineffective at preventing placement. But the Illinois program did not follow the Homebuilders model. In fact, the very study these critics cite as showing the Illinois programs didn't prevent placement, also reveals that Illinois took every rule for how to run a successful family preservation program and broke it. To cite just a few examples:

- The average caseload in the Illinois program was nearly double the maximum permitted under Homebuilders. As a result, workers in this so-called intensive program spent an average of only 32.4 minutes per day with a family.
- Provision of ongoing services after the "family preservation" intervention was "haphazard and inadequate."
- Agencies providing the services were allowed to lower their hiring standards.

And, it is important to note that when even this program was effectively abandoned, child abuse deaths went up, not down.

And the study itself was little better than the program examined. A rigorous review of the methodology of several such studies found that the Illinois study was among the very worst. In contrast, according to one of the nation's leading IFPS researchers, Prof. Ray Kirk of the University of North Carolina School of Social Work: "There is a growing body of evidence that IFPS works, in that it is more effective than traditional services in preventing out-of-home placements of children in high-risk families."

Some critics argue that evaluations of family preservation programs are inherently flawed because they allegedly focus on placement prevention instead of child safety. But a placement can only be prevented if a child is believed to be safe. Placement prevention *is* a measure of safety.

Of course, the key words here are "believed to be." Children who have been through intensive family preservation programs are generally among the most closely monitored. But there are cases in which children are reabused and nobody finds out. And there are cases in which the warnings of family preservation workers are ignored. No one can be absolutely certain that the child left at home is safe—but no one can be absolutely certain that the child placed in foster care is safe either—and family preservation has the better track record.

Indeed, the whole idea that family preservation—and only family preservation—should be required to prove itself over and over again reflects a double standard. After more than a century of experience, isn't it time that the advocates of foster care be held to account for the failure of their program? . . .

Family Preservation and Adoption

Critics of family preservation claim that it makes it harder to free children for adoption. Once again, they are wrong.

Not only does family preservation not impede adoption, family preservation can speed the process of terminating parental rights when necessary.

The federal law that effectively abolished reasonable efforts also requires states to seek termination of parental rights for almost any child in foster care for 15 of the most recent 22 months. Yet in many jurisdictions it can take at least 12 months for a judge to decide if the initial placement was justified in the first place. And this influx of new termination cases comes despite increasing evidence that the system can't cope with the thousands of children legally free for adoption right now.

Highly touted figures showing a large percentage increase in adoptions leave out crucial information. Though large in percentage terms, in real numbers the annual increase is less than 1.1 percent of the total number of children in foster care on any given day. That was all states could manage, even though the federal government offers them a huge financial incentive—$4,000 to $6,000 for every adoption over a baseline number—and political and media pressure for adoption is enormous. In contrast, since 1985 the foster care population has increased by an average of 5 percent a year. The real message from the so-called surge in adoptions is that the problems of foster care can never be solved through adoption alone.

Furthermore, the figures include only finalized adoptions, not the number of cases in which parental rights were terminated, but no adoptive home was found. A 1997 study found that fewer than one third of the children legally free for adoption in 1996 actually were adopted. In another study, Prof. Martin Guggenheim of New York University Law School examined two states which have expedited termination proceedings. He found that as the number of children freed for adoption soared, the number of actual adoptions increased far more slowly. The result: A generation of legal orphans, who have no ties whatsoever to their birth parents, but aren't being placed for adoption either. Guggenheim found that, contrary to the unsupported rhetoric of critics of family preservation, the one reform taken most seriously since the 1970s has been termination of parental rights. The pattern is repeating itself in New Jersey, where between 1997 and 1999 almost four children had parental rights terminated for every one actually adopted. And a study of urban counties in Nebraska found that more than a year after parental rights were terminated, fewer than half the children had permanent homes.

Even if all the children now awaiting adoption could be placed, that doesn't mean the placements will last. Current efforts to plunge headlong into adoption are being undertaken in the absence of any reliable data about how often placements "disrupt" when parents who adopt a child—especially a "special needs" child—change their minds.

But the evidence we do have is alarming. Already, officials in several states are estimating that between 15 and 25 percent of so-called "forever families" don't turn out to be forever after all—the adoptive parents change their minds.

That number is only likely to increase as workers feel pressure to cash in on the bounties for adoptive placements called for in the new federal law—bounties which are paid whether the adoption actually lasts or not.

One Washington State agency that places "special needs" children took special precautions to prevent the adoptions from disrupting: It hired the Homebuilders family preservation program to preserve the adoptive families. But if current efforts to smear family preservation succeed even as more children are thrown into adoptive placements with little thought or planning, there won't be nearly enough programs like Homebuilders around to help all the adoptive families who need them.

There are other reasons why the best way to ensure more adoptions is to have a strong family preservation program. Michigan has the largest family preservation program in America. It also has an outstanding record for getting foster children adopted.

"There is definitely a connection between whether enough is done on the front end and whether you can terminate parental rights," says Susan Carter, former Executive Director of the National Association of Foster Care Reviewers. "If the judge knows that everything has been done properly [to try to preserve the family] but it failed, he will feel better that at least he is making the right choice."

The Substitute Care Fantasy

The argument that there are children trapped in foster care who should be adopted and the argument that there are children trapped in foster care who should be in their own homes are not mutually exclusive. There are children in foster care who should be exiting in both directions.

But the claim that family preservation impedes adoption is nonsense. So is the claim that it was extremely difficult to terminate parental rights before the law was changed. All that is needed is minimal competence on the part of child protective workers. . . .

We have always believed there is a place for efforts to increase the number of adoptions as part of child welfare reform. But as long as the rush to cash in on adoption bounties causes a further neglect of efforts to keep families in their own homes, it will only make things worse.

Contrary to critics' claims, most people in child protection work are almost obsessed with a substitute care fantasy, in which children are rescued from their "evil" birth parents and placed in substitute settings, which, in the imagination of the workers, are always ideal. For most workers and most agencies, termination of parental rights is the dessert in the child welfare meal, family preservation is the broccoli. The new federal law gives workers and agencies all the dessert they want without ensuring that they eat their broccoli first.

*"Child welfare's preoccupation with
preserving biological families has meant
more reliance on foster care, not less."*

Policies Should Not Emphasize Family Preservation

Amanda Spake

In 1997, Congress enacted the Adoption and Safe Families Act in an attempt to move more children into adoptive families and out of foster care and abusive homes. The ASFA implemented a number of changes to encourage adoption among foster children instead of reuniting them with their families. In the following viewpoint, Amanda Spake asserts that policies must create more adoption opportunities for children in foster care. Spake asserts that child welfare agencies must not give precedence to factors such as race and kinship when placing foster children in adoptive homes. In addition, she argues that efforts to reunify families must not be required when there is an immediate threat to the child's safety. Spake is a senior writer at the *Washington Post* and a former editor of *Mother Jones*.

As you read, consider the following questions:
1. How have efforts to reunify biological families obstructed adoptions, according to Spake?
2. According to the author, what are the average characteristics of kin caregivers?
3. In Spake's opinion, what measures has Project Hustle taken to succeed in meeting permanency goals for hard-to-place children?

As many as 200,000 American kids languish in foster care, waiting to be adopted. But the barriers to public adoption are so great that even a president's vow and a new law will not be enough to find them homes

Ten years ago, Dede Van Zandt and her husband, Keith, a physician, decided to adopt another child. The North Carolina couple already had three children, but they wanted a larger family, and they'd heard that infants and young kids, many with medical conditions linked to prenatal exposure to drugs or alcohol, were swelling the foster care ranks in their state, as in others.

The Van Zandts applied at several public and private agencies to adopt special-needs children. But to their surprise and disappointment, they were told they'd have a very long wait. Only African-American children were available, they were told. Even though they made clear that as white parents they would be happy to adopt a black child, no one took them up on their offer. "We knew they'd never place them with us," says Dede Van Zandt.

Two years passed. The Van Zandts contacted child welfare agencies in other states, with no success. Finally, they gave up on adopting an American child. In April 1991, they left for Bucharest to pick up 5-week-old Hannah, and two years later they went back to adopt Annie, a 4-year-old Romanian orphan with serious medical and emotional problems. "We felt forced to go overseas," Dede Van Zandt says. "We knew the kids were here but we couldn't get at them."

The kids are indeed here. On any given day in the United States, at least 107,000 of the 507,000 children currently in foster care are waiting for adoption, according to the Child Welfare League of America. More than 100,000 other children are likely to need adoptive homes after attempts to reunite them with their biological families fail.

A Small Percentage Find Homes

Chances are, however, that only a small percentage of these needy children will find new homes. Despite the abundance of available children, adoptions from public agencies have for more than a decade remained at about 20,000 per year—a number that makes up only 16 percent of the 125,000 children adopted in the United States in 1997. In contrast, private adoptions, arranged through agencies or lawyers, account for 35 percent of U.S. adoptions, at a cost of $10,000 to $30,000 per child. And Americans in 1997 adopted 13,620 children from overseas, 35 percent more than in 1988.

The disparity between the number of kids in foster care who need homes and the number who are adopted spurred President Clinton in 1996 to ask for new legislation aimed at doubling the number of public adoptions by 2002 and giving foster children "what should be their fundamental right—a chance at a decent, safe home." In response, Congress in November 1997 passed the Adoption and Safe Families Act, designed to increase public adoptions and to speed up the adoption process. And in June 1998 the Department of Health and Human Services held a forum in Washington, D.C., to assist state officials, juvenile court judges, and administrators to implement the new law at the local level.

Yet even with the new law, it may be years before the political and bureaucratic obstacles to public adoption are reduced to the point that the number increases dramatically. The middle class has largely abandoned public adoption in favor of less difficult alternatives—a reality no legal shift can soon remedy. And in most states, adoption has not been the top priority of public child welfare agencies. Instead, for more than 30 years the focus has been on preserving troubled birth families and addressing the needs of a burgeoning foster care population. When it comes to the needs of children, these agencies have tended to give issues of race and kinship precedence over placing kids in adoptive homes. The long-term result is that thousands of children have spent their childhoods in temporary homes, while families like the Van Zandts, who might want to adopt them, grow so frustrated that they give up altogether on adopting American children.

Child Welfare's Preoccupation

Children who have stable, predictable care "can overcome great adversity," says Richard Gelles, director of the Family Violence Research Program at the University of Rhode Island and an architect of the Adoption and Safe Families Act. Conversely, adults who grow up in temporary homes often suffer: Studies have shown that anywhere from 15 percent to 56 percent never complete high school or earn a GED. The majority hold low-skilled jobs; up to 50 percent spend some time on public assistance. Drug use is common. Nearly one third of males commit crimes as adults. Among the homeless, as many as 39 percent spent years in foster care as kids.

Despite this grim picture, child welfare's preoccupation with preserving biological families has meant more reliance on foster care, not less. The Adoption Assistance and Child Welfare Act of 1980 required states receiving federal funds to make "reasonable efforts" to reunite kids with their birth parents. "Reasonable" was never defined. "The law was passed to prevent 'foster care drift,'" says Ann Sullivan of the Child Welfare League. Instead, the law created it. . . .

Keeping these kids stuck in temporary homes is not only devastating to the kids—it has been a fiscal disaster. The federal payment for foster care, 55 percent of the total, grew 438 percent in the past decade to about $3.5 billion in 1998. Foster care's payment structure actually discourages adoption—the more kids in foster care, the more money states get from the federal government for their overall programs, since 50 percent of foster care funds go to administrative costs, including social worker salaries. A 1993 study estimated that the adoption of 40,700 kids between 1983 and 1987 saved $1.6 billion in taxpayer dollars—mostly in administrative costs.

"Reasonable Efforts"

Legal interpretations of the "reasonable efforts" required to reunify families also have posed a major impediment to adoption. "When we were working to get the 1980 law passed, we talked about a cascade of services to preserve families," says the National Council for Adoption's William Pierce. "We had no idea that judges would mandate exhaustive efforts at every step." In a 1982 case, the U.S. Supreme Court ruled that a state agency's "first obligation" is to offer services to preserve any biological family whose children have been taken into foster care. Before terminating the parents' rights, the court held, a state must show that after the child entered care "diligent efforts" were made to strengthen the family—and that the birth parents failed "substantially and continuously" to maintain contact with or plan for the child, though physically and financially able to do so. Attempting to prove the child was "neglected" with less than "clear and convincing evidence," the court ruled, was a violation of the birth parents' due-process rights.

Altering Our Approach

The Adoption and Safe Families Act . . . fundamentally alters our Nation's approach to foster care and adoption. And fundamentally, it will improve the well-being of hundreds of thousands of our most vulnerable children. The new legislation makes it clear that children's health and safety are the paramount concerns of our public child welfare system. It makes it clear that good foster care provides important safe havens for our children, but it is by definition a temporary, not a permanent, setting.

Bill Clinton, *Weekly Compilation of Presidential Documents*, November 24, 1997.

The much-publicized story of Laura Blankman's failed attempt to adopt her 2-year-old foster son, Cornilous Pixley, is just one example of how far courts have gone to preserve birth parents' interests. Blankman, a Montgomery County, Md., police officer, has cared for Cornilous since he was 2 weeks old. Yet a Maryland judge ruled that the boy should be returned to his biological mother, 24-year-old Latrena Pixley, with whom he has had limited contact. Pixley was convicted in 1993 of smothering her 6-week-old daughter, Cornilous's half sister. The judge's decision was greeted with national outrage, yet he maintained his hands were tied by state law: Pixley's murder conviction, he said, did not constitute the special circumstances required to terminate her parental rights. Maryland's Court of Special Appeals is expected to rule on Blankman's appeal.

Recently, family preservation efforts have extended beyond parents to include other blood relatives. Twenty-one states and the 1996 federal welfare law give a child's kin priority in foster placements. Nationally, about 23 percent of foster kids are in kinship care; in urban areas and among African-American kids, the number is greater.

"Kids in kinship care stay in the child welfare system,"

says Peter Digre, director of children and family services for Los Angeles County. "Kin don't adopt." Family dynamics often make relatives reluctant to adopt: Grandparents, for example, may not want to displace their adult child by terminating parental rights. Money may also be a motivating factor. Kinship care is less costly and thus more attractive than traditional foster care in states that have a two-tier foster payment structure: Nonrelative foster parents receive an average of $612 per month per child; kinship caregivers receive an amount equal to public assistance, $375 per month for a family of three. Both amounts are higher than the federal subsidy paid to families adopting special-needs children, an average of $230 per month. There is no subsidy for adopted children who do not have special needs.

Many kin caregivers rely on the additional income foster kids generate. They tend to be older than other foster parents—two thirds are grandparents—and less educated: 43 percent dropped out of high school. More than half of kin caregivers—58 percent—are jobless, and nearly 39 percent live in poverty.

The Current Wisdom

The current wisdom in child welfare is that Americans have fled public adoption because the kids in foster care are not those prospective parents want. If adoptive parents "could have adopted a healthy white infant in this country, they would not have gone overseas," says Gloria Hochman of the National Adoption Center, a federally funded group that maintains a registry of adoptable U.S. kids.

But while history may back up Hochman's claim, statistics show that foreign adoptees share more characteristics with U.S. foster kids than many people realize. Only 38 percent of those adopted abroad in 1997, for example, could be called "white." The majority, 62 percent, were children of color from Asia, Central and South America, the Caribbean, and Africa. Similarly, 55 percent of adoptable U.S. kids are minorities, four-fifths of whom are African-American; 45 percent are "white." In a recent informal survey of the 1,400-member Families for Russian and Ukrainian Adoption, a key reason parents cited for adopting abroad was

"Tried and failed under the U.S. system (including being rejected as parents for cross-racial adoptions).". . . .

Race does have an impact on many Americans' decision to seek foreign adoption—in part because some social workers don't want to place black kids with white parents. "We tend to treat kids as belonging in a propertylike way to their blood parents and to their racial groups," says Harvard law professor Elizabeth Bartholet, an expert on adoption and race. "The overwhelming emphasis of the system has been on where people came from rather than where they're going. It defines kids by their past, not by their futures." The fact is that many white couples want minority children, but social workers have been uncomfortable with transracial adoptions since the National Association of Black Social Workers termed them "genocide" in 1972. Though NABSW has softened its opposition, transracial adoptions still account for only 4 percent of all adoptions, according to the Child Welfare League.

Yet the only long-term studies of transracial adoption, by American University sociologist Rita Simon, show that rather than being erased, racial identity is openly discussed in transracial families and so is adoption, since transracial adoptees cannot escape the knowledge that they are adopted. Kids report that they must make major adjustments growing up in a mixed-race family, but many say that contrary to the arguments that they will be stranded between two worlds and part of neither, their upbringing allows them to operate freely in black and white cultures. . . .

The distaste for transracial adoption in social welfare circles, however, has strengthened efforts to recruit minorities as adoptive parents. . . . But even if such recruitment efforts meet their goals completely, there will still be a shortage of homes for the thousands of African-American kids who are waiting, according to research by Richard Barth at the University of California, Berkeley.

And the longer African-American children are forced to wait for homes, the less likely it is they will ever have them. In a study of nearly 4,000 California children in foster care, Barth found that six years after foster placement, only 11 percent of the white children but 33 percent of the African-American kids were still in the system. White children were five times as likely to be adopted as African-American kids of the same age, in part because there are always more white parents to be "matched" with adoptable kids. Another survey of 900 adoptive families, however, indicated that 40 percent would be interested in adopting children of other races—if such kids were made available to them.

Age is also a key factor in a child's chance of adoption, and it's often related to race. Infants are four times as likely to be adopted as older children. An African-American infant has the same chance of adoption as a white preschooler. But a black child trapped in the system until age 7 or 8 may never be adopted—delay amounts to de facto racial discrimination.

Many adoptive parents fear that older children cannot bond. Attachment disorder has become the boogeyman of adoption, says Alicia Lieberman, director of the Child Trauma Research Project at San Francisco General Hospital, a misunderstanding "that locates the source of the problem in the child, rather than in the child's relationships.". . .

Finding enough families who really believe in these kids will not happen overnight. The Adoption and Safe Families Act will help to some extent, by encouraging states to devote more resources to adoption and by placing time limits on family reunification. The act limits family preservation delays by requiring a permanent plan for each foster child within 12 months.

Real Success in Texas

Real success, however, may come only when the states themselves initiate new approaches to family recruitment and develop strategies for cutting through public adoption's avalanche of red tape. No state is making more of these efforts than Texas. And one of the secrets of Texas's success is Helen Grape, regional placement program director for the state's Department of Protective and Regulatory Services in Fort Worth.

A stylish woman, in touch with offices, social workers, and parents via a cell phone seemingly grown into her ear, Grape is the force behind Project Hustle, an adoption program for hard-to-place kids that has become a national model. Project Hustle's kids have physical or mental handicaps or are members of large sibling groups. Nearly all are minorities, and most have been waiting over a year for a family. Project Hustle teams—made up of community groups, adoptive parents, minority adoption councils, churches, and others—are assigned 20 to 25 children. Their mission is to network their way to the right families for these kids. To cut through bureaucratic delays, a few caseworkers drop other tasks and become "adoption specialists," making sure the paperwork moves through the system once families are found. To make Hustle work, Grape says, "Basically, we had to change the way we did almost everything." In its first five months, four Project Hustle teams got 85 kids adopted.

Child welfare was not always like this in Texas. Just three years ago, children spent an average of 40.8 months in the system awaiting adoption. Children in foster care were moved four times or more and stayed 44 months. "This had to stop," says Hal Gaither, a juvenile court judge in Dallas. The judge, a West Point graduate in snakeskin cowboy boots who claims to play "a mean guitar," got tough. "In Dallas, we started saying these cases are going to be tried in six months." No continuances were allowed. Last year, more than 95 percent of child protective cases in Dallas went to a final hearing in 12 months. "I know of no other state moving faster," says Gaither. With the support of Governor George W. Bush, Gaither took his ideas to the Legislature in Austin. On January 1, 1998, "12 months and out" became law.

The Texas law conforms to 1997's Adoption and Safe Families Act, and adds extra enforcement. Among families with records of severe mistreatment of kids, family preservation efforts are not required. The federal act offers a "bounty" for each child a state places for adoption over the number placed the previous year. Agencies are required to terminate birth parents' rights and begin adoption for any child who's been in foster care 15 out of the preceding 22 months. In addition, the Multiethnic Placement Act, passed in 1994 and toughened in 1996, bans racial discrimination in foster and adoptive placements. In Texas, social workers can be fired for failing to abide by MEPA.

There is hope in Texas that the state's adoption-friendly system and rapid response to the new laws will bring a younger, middle-class group of parents back to public adoption.

> *"Internet photolisting of children . . . has the potential to expand the pool of families available for the children."*

The Internet Should Be Used to Recruit Adoptive Families

Children's Bureau

The Children's Bureau (CB) is the oldest federal child welfare agency, located within the U.S. Department of Health and Human Services. In the following viewpoint, the CB contends that the Internet can be a valuable tool to link adoptable children with available families. This organization insists that "photolisting" children on adoption websites will help match them with adoptive families more quickly and will communicate the growing need for adoption to a wider audience. Responding to issues of potential child exploitation and invasion of privacy, the CB makes recommendations on how to protect the safety and confidentiality of children photolisted for adoption on the Internet.

As you read, consider the following questions:

1. What demographics of Internet users does the CB cite to support its assertion that the Internet is a valuable resource for adoption?
2. In the author's opinion, which children should be listed for adoption on the Internet?
3. According to the CB, what procedures are taken to protect the privacy and confidentiality of adoptable children advertised on television or in newspapers?

Reprinted from "Plan to Implement a National Internet Adoption Photolisting Service," published by the Children's Bureau of the U.S. Department of Health and Human Services at www.acf.dhhs.gov/programs/cb/initiatives/photolts/toc.htm.

Nationwide, approximately 520,000 children are in State foster care systems. Of those who exit these systems, three out of four are reunified with their parents or other relatives. For children who cannot return home safely, it is important to find alternative permanent homes. This has been historically difficult to arrange because many of these children are school age, have physical or mental impairments, belong to sibling groups or are of minority heritage. In brief, they are children with special needs.

The latest information available from the Adoption and Foster Care Analysis and Reporting System (AFCARS) indicates that there are about 110,000 children in the public child welfare system who have a permanency goal of adoption and/or whose parents' parental rights have been terminated. State AFCARS data indicate that about 37,000 children are actually free for adoption. Of the children free for adoption, over 35 percent are teenagers and about 17 percent are between the ages of 9 and 12 years. Two-thirds of the children have been in care for two years or more and almost 30 percent have been in care for more than five years. African-Americans make up 48 percent of the population, 33 percent are white and 11 percent are of Hispanic origin.

Frequently, children in the child welfare system are adopted by either their foster parents or relatives. We estimate that approximately 64 percent will be adopted by their foster families and another 14 percent will be adopted by relatives. This means that of the 37,000 children who are free and available for adoption, 29,000 will probably be or are in the process of being adopted by their foster parents or by relatives, which leaves about 8,000 children who are legally free and available for adoption and for whom adoptive families need to be identified.

A Valuable Tool

As the States implement the provisions of the Adoption and Safe Families Act over the next several years, many expect that more children will have a permanency goal of adoption and will become free and available for adoption more rapidly than before. Thus, the numbers of children for whom adoptive families need to be found will continue to increase. In order to find families for these children, the Internet will be a valuable tool. . . .

Various studies and surveys estimate the current number of Internet users to be between 50 and 60 million while some projections indicate that there will be almost 150 million users by the year 2002. Recent news releases indicate that the Internet will become even more accessible, without the burden of owning or learning how to use a computer. Users will be able to surf the web on home television via satellite dish or cable TV without needing or using the standard computer hookup. While there are no hard and fast data on which everyone can agree concerning the overall demographics of the population of Internet users, there seems to be consensus that racially and ethnically it mirrors quite closely the general population. Adult users tend to be somewhat better educated than the general population and have higher average earnings. The number of actual and potential users together with the latest advances in the technology indicate the current and potential value of the Internet as a resource for providing information about adoption and for finding permanent homes for adoptive special needs children.

A recent survey indicates that 37 States have already developed their own adoption photolisting sites on the Internet that can be accessed by the general public. These Internet sites can provide agencies with leads for follow-up activities with interested inquirers. One State indicates that most of the families who inquire about a child through the Internet are already approved to adopt a child or are in the process of approval, which makes it easier to move toward adoption. . . .

Recruiting Families

Every State recruits families and places children for adoption. They have regularly used radio and television spots and advertisements, billboards, newspaper articles, special events, booths at fairs and other innovative activities. Most States place children on State, regional and national exchanges. Over time, additional methods of recruitment have been developed such as the Internet photolisting of children which extends recruitment efforts beyond States' geographical boundaries and has the potential to expand the pool of families available for the children. Finalizing an adoption requires myriad activities with major cooperation from both the public and private sectors. . . .

Nothing Illegal or Unethical

There is nothing that is illegal or even unethical about an adoption broker or facilitator having a Web site. Some very ethical and mainstream adoption agencies have Web sites. The question is if this particular Web site defrauded people. The only thing that makes it unique is the Web's distribution and availability means there are potentially more victims.

Charles Feldman, *CNN News*, January 17, 2001.

During the past two decades a great deal of attention has been focused on finding permanent homes for children free for adoption in the child welfare system. The Federal Adoption Opportunities Discretionary Grants Program led the way to removing barriers to adoption of children with special needs and it continues to provide support to public and private agencies for adoption demonstrations. The private sector has also been instrumental in developing and implementing grants and providing other financial support to facilitate placements for children with special needs. The efforts of the private sector have for the most part utilized traditional methods of recruiting adoptive families such as photolisting books, adoption fairs, and broadcast and print media. However, some initiatives have utilized the technology of photolisting children on the Internet, such as the National Adoption Exchange and Faces of Adoption:

- The National Adoption Exchange (NAE) is a secure membership-based Internet system run by the National Adoption Center and funded by the Department since 1983. The grant to the Center is funded at $500,000 per year. . . . It uses the Internet for its exchange, lists both children who are available for adoption and registered families who have been approved to adopt. It allows exchanges, public and private agencies, adoption professionals, and adoptive parent groups nationwide to work together via the World Wide Web. For the quarter ending October 1998, the NAE listed 700 approved adoptive families and 3,091 children from 42 States. The NAE is not available to the public.

- Faces of Adoption (FACES) is a national Internet pho-tolisting service that brings children "online" through photographs and descriptions and offers a wealth of in-formation on its website to assist potential adoptive parents. FACES, unlike the NAE, is open to the public [and] lists only children not families. . . . FACES was initially funded in 1995 by a Federal Adoption Oppor-tunities grant to the National Adoption Center (NAC) and is now supported by the Dave Thomas Foundation for Adoption. According to a report from FACES, there has been a dramatic increase in States' usage of the Center's website since the passage of the Adoption and Safe Families Act of 1997. FACES' experience in Internet photolisting technology provided valuable in-formation for developing this report and is evidence that the Internet will provide a much wider audience with information on adoption and on children waiting for placement. FACES photolists an average of 1200 children. To date, 71 children have been placed with adoptive families as a result of photolisting children online.

During the latter part of December 1998, FACES and 26 States with Internet photolisting systems (of the 37 States known to have such sites) responded to an informal survey by the National Adoption Information Clearinghouse to learn about their experiences on using the Internet to pho-tolist waiting children. All but two States found the Internet photolisting to be a good recruitment tool. The other two States were non-committal. A large percentage of the re-spondents stated that the Internet expanded the pool of fam-ilies who have approved homestudies and others viewed it as the best possible tool for public education on adoption. Ev-ery State saw an increase in the inquiries about adoption, but not necessarily about special needs children. . . .

The Need for Internet Photolisting

Information from the American Public Human Services As-sociation (APHSA) indicates that 47 States are using the Internet as a cross-jurisdictional resource to find adoptive families for waiting children. This is being done through a combination of State and regional services or nationally through the NAE and FACES. The regional exchanges and the NAE list both children and prospective adoptive families, but these listings are only accessible to workers and adoptive parent groups in the member States. The social workers use the listings on the exchanges to look for prospective adoptive parents for the children in the custody of the State or agency in which they work; they spend little or no time looking for children who can be appropriately placed with a given prospective adoptive parent. Other than the staff of the NAE and Adopt America, there are probably very few individuals or social workers who actually look for special needs children for prospective adoptive parents. The State photolisting sites and FACES are available to the general public and therefore to prospective adoptive parents themselves to search for children they might adopt.

It is suggested that a national Internet photolisting service be implemented and that after a period of full operation, three to five years, its efficiency and effectiveness be fully evaluated. There are other Internet photolisting sites—the National Adoption Exchange, FACES, and State and regional services. The NAE is, however, not accessible by individual prospective adoptive parents. FACES, the other national service, includes only 1,200 children. The backing, financial and organizational, of the Federal government would facilitate the creation of a larger Internet photolisting service open to the public. The Federal photolisting service could potentially include the 7,000 to 8,000 children who are now legally free for adoption and who will likely not be adopted by their foster families or relatives. Federal participation would be critical to assembling all the interested parties and building a consensus regarding potentially contentious issues such as privacy and time frames for responding to inquiries about particular children. A standardized format would be used for listing of these children on the Federal service, as opposed to the range of formats used for (and the variation in information provided by) the existing photolisting services. . . .

Which Children Should Be Listed?

Currently, States and adoption exchanges such as FACES list only children who are legally free and immediately available for adoption and who have special needs conditions which makes them harder to place. However, it should be noted that the majority of children who meet these criteria are *not* listed on the Internet because they are in the process of being adopted by their foster parents or by relatives, and therefore additional recruitment of families on their behalf is not required.

In identifying which children should be listed, other issues have been raised that might affect the above criteria. For example, some State courts are reluctant to free children for adoption until a family is located. Because States and courts have varying laws and policies on this, the consultation work group [the group responsible for developing recommendations for the implementation of a national photolisting service] needs to explore whether consideration for listing on the Internet should be made for exceptions such as:

- when a petition for termination of parental rights is in the court system and close to resolution; or
- the court or birth family refuses to free the child unless an adoptive family has been found.

If these children are placed on the Internet, information about their circumstances must be included in the photolisting material. . . .

Privacy and Confidentiality

Newspaper and television news reports are carrying more stories each day indicating how computers and access to the Internet are facilitating undesired access to personal and supposedly private confidential information such as bank accounts, health information, drivers' license data, buying habits or other less obvious activities. Regarding the adoption photolisting initiative, specific concern has been expressed about a child's confidential or identifying information becoming accessible to the public, or to hackers or classmates or even, possibly, to child molesters.

Television programs such as "Wednesday's Child," the "Children Awaiting Placement" photolisting books used by

States to feature children waiting for adoption, the States' own photolisting activities and the NAE's FACES have all been providing interested people with information about prospective adoptees. Each of these services is concerned about confidentiality and privacy and has developed procedures and conventions that are designed to provide information about prospective adoptees with minimal risk. A cursory review of their procedures does not indicate any misuse of the information or breaches of the systems. Some of their procedures include the following:

- Use first names only of children,
- Do not identify the child's locality of birth or residence,
- Do not give the child's specific birth date,
- Do not give any information about the child's parents,
- Keep descriptions about handicapping conditions generic, and
- Use a specific identifying number for referencing the child and tracking him/her back to the State agency.

It is suggested that experts in the area of privacy and confidentiality both from within and outside the Department be included as members of the consultation work group. It is also suggested that there be a thorough, detailed analysis of the privacy, confidentiality and safety impact—including technical, human, and organizational aspects—of placing information about children available for adoption on the Internet. It would include a study of past experiences to identify any types of possible misuse of information and estimates of magnitude of risk, and would evaluate the procedures and conventions now in use. Based on the results of this analysis, it is further suggested that national standards be developed about what types of information should be made available on the Internet to assure the privacy, confidentiality and the safety of the prospective adoptees.

"[Internet] facilitators appear to be working in a gray area where . . . there is frequently little oversight from local authorities."

Internet Adoption Remains a Gray Area

Frances Grandy Taylor

In the following viewpoint, Frances Grandy Taylor contends that Internet adoptions may leave adoptive couples vulnerable to fraud. Taylor argues that while many Internet adoption websites are reputable, the Internet has allowed many unscrupulous adoption brokers to exploit hopeful couples. Because of the anonymity of the Internet, many brokers simply shut down their websites and start their businesses in another state. She insists that until adoption facilitators are federally regulated, unethical adoption brokers will be permitted to operate. Taylor is a staff writer at the *Hartford Courant*, a daily Connecticut newspaper.

As you read, consider the following questions:
1. Why does Taylor claim that Internet facilitators operate within a "gray area"?
2. According to Penny Rearick, how do facilitators find couples that are desperate to adopt?
3. What "red flags" should prospective adoptive parents look for when using the Internet?

The Internet is making couples seeking to adopt more vulnerable to deception and disappointment.

While many legitimate and established agencies are using the Web to attract and identify potential adoptive parents, they are operating side by side with fly-by-night facilitators who request thousands of dollars in fees and then disappear.

A Gray Area

These facilitators appear to be working in a gray area where the adoption regulations vary in each state, and there is frequently little oversight from local authorities.

"Many couples have been through infertility, and in some cases these facilitators find their names on Internet message boards and contact them," said Penny Rearick, executive director of Adoption Resource of Connecticut. "These people are often very desperate."

The Internet has made it easier for couples seeking babies and babies available for adoption to find each other. There are Web sites that specialize in foreign adoption from such countries as Russia or China; others are aimed at birth mothers who may be considering adoption. Agencies like the state Department of Children and Families (DCF) have Web sites that include photo listings of children available for adoption.

Rearick, who has helped several families in the state when an adoption has gone awry, said many of the unethical facilitators operate in California and other states with loose adoption laws.

Connecticut has some of the most stringent adoption laws in the country. Any adoption agency operating in this state must be licensed by the DCF. Couples who adopt without using an agency must undergo a home study by a state-licensed agency, and the adoption must be finalized in probate court.

An agency or facilitator who is acting illegally could have its license suspended by the DCF, said Thomas Gilman, deputy commissioner, and any violation of criminal laws could be referred to the state attorney general's office.

"My advice to prospective parents is to use a licensed agency and to check them out," Gilman said. "Do your homework. This is one of the most important decisions you will ever make. Adoptions are expensive, but if someone is asking for an exorbitant amount of money, it should raise suspicions."

In the case of the 7-month-old twin girls involved in an international custody battle, it appears they may have been offered on the Internet to two previous couples before being adopted by Richard and Vickie Allen of California. The girls were taken back by their birth mother, Tranda Wecker of St. Louis, Missouri, and adopted again days later by Judith and Alan Kilshaw of Wales. The babies have been put in foster care until the matter goes before a judge in England. The birth father has filed for custody of the twins. [The twins were returned to the United States, where an Arkansas judge denied both the Kilshaws and the Allens custody of Kimberly and Belinda. They are currently living in foster care. Tranda Wecker has petitioned for their custody as well.]

State Attorney General Richard Blumenthal said his office has not encountered a similar case in this state, but disputes have arisen due to carelessness, not fraud, on the part of an agency.

On a Broader Scale

"This kind of intentional fraud or deception does not seem to be common," Blumenthal said. "The Internet always raises the specter of fraud on a broader scale. There is certainly grave jeopardy when the Internet is used in this kind of a significant transaction." The Adoption Resource Center of Connecticut does not place children for adoption but helps families who wish to adopt find reputable agencies and helps families involved in international adoption through the maze of paperwork and regulations.

"If someone promises that you can build a family in four months, that is a huge red flag. That's just not reality. Adoption takes longer than that most of the time," Rearick said. Beware of anyone who offers a baby before a home study has been initiated or completed.

"Be careful of someone who offers references. One thing that is becoming more common is people being paid to act as references," Rearick said. "There should be a social worker who works with the birth parent and someone working with the adoptive family. There should never be one person counseling both parties. It's a huge conflict of interest. That's also a red flag."

"Be sure you have a written contract before you give anyone any money. There should be a provision in there for how much money you get back if the adoption doesn't happen. Otherwise, you could be out thousands of dollars and still not have a baby."

Mary Lib Mooney, a Lexington, Virginia, mother of three, has a Web site, theadoptionguide.com, which enables users to find out about complaints against adoption agencies and other information. Mooney and her husband were victims of a failed Russian adoption in 1996. They settled out of court with the North Carolina agency that handled the adoption.

"I don't really think Internet adoption is bad. It has more advantages than disadvantages. Because of the Internet, it's now easier to find agencies in other states or the kind of adoption you want," Mooney said. "It also exposes you to more unscrupulous people than before."

Mooney said Tina Johnson, the San Diego adoption broker in the twins case who appears to have gone underground, is operating in a gray area—she is allowed to charge fees for her services, state laws differ and there are no federal regulations regarding adoption.

"She can blame the whole thing on the birth mother," Mooney said. "All she'll do is change her name and pop up in a different state and start the whole thing all over again."

Mooney and others say the need for federal regulations for adoption are long overdue and would help reduce fraud. "Until then, it's wide open for the Tina Johnsons of the world."

Periodical Bibliography

The following articles have been selected to supplement the diverse views presented in this chapter. Addresses are provided for periodicals not indexed in the *Readers' Guide to Periodical Literature*, the *Alternative Press Index*, the *Social Sciences Index*, or the *Index to Legal Periodicals and Books*.

Christian Science
Monitor
"A Law Changes, a Birth Mother Worries," *Christian Science Monitor*, April 17, 2000.

Richard J. Gelles
"The Adoption and Safe Families Act of 1997 Rightly Places Child Safety First," *Brown University Child and Adolescent Behavior Letter*, April 1998. Available from Mantisses Communications Group, 208 Governor St., Providence, RI 02906.

Susan Greene
"Online Adoption Sparks Debate," *Denver Post*, April 13, 1999.

Martha Groves
"Open Adoption, Which Keeps the Birth Parents in the Loop, Is Becoming Common Even Among the Formerly Skeptical," *Los Angeles Times*, August 8, 1999.

Tamar Lewin
"At Core of Adoption Dispute Is Crazy Quilt of State Laws," *New York Times*, January 19, 2001.

Laura Mansnerus
"Market Puts Price Tags on the Priceless," *New York Times*, October 26, 1998.

Art Moore and
Christine J. Gardner
"Can Foster Care Be Fixed: Churches Partner with Parents to Care For At-Risk Children," *Christianity Today*, August 10, 1998.

Time
"Tracking Down Mom: Should Adopted Children Have the Right to Uncover Their Birth Parents? More States Are Trying to Open the Records," *Time*, February 22, 1999.

Sam Howe Vernick
"An Adoptee-Rights Hero Who Knows All the Arguments," *New York Times*, June 3, 2000.

Cheryl Weitzstein
"Adoption Advocates Encouraged by Big Response to Internet Sites," *Insight on the News*, February 2, 1998. Available from 3600 New York Ave. NE, Washington, DC 20002.

For Further Discussion

Chapter 1

1. Evelyn Burns Robinson maintains that adoption is a permanent solution to temporary problems that families face. What problems does Robinson address? Elizabeth Bartholet insists that adoption is the best option for children who cannot return to their troubled families. What problems of these families does Bartholet discuss? How do the problems that the authors discuss differ? In your opinion, who addresses the more important problems? Explain your answer.

2. Marvin Olasky argues that the biased media do not portray adoption as a viable alternative to abortion and single-parenting. Meanwhile, Katha Pollitt claims that the media romanticize adoption and promote it as an alternative to abortion. In your opinion, who makes the more compelling argument? Why?

Chapter 2

1. Heather Lowe contends that many prospective birth mothers are influenced by biased child placement professionals to place their children for adoption. In your opinion, is Lowe for or against adoption? Provide examples from the reading.

2. This chapter presents the specific rights of birth mothers, birth fathers, adoptive parents, and adopted children that adoption advocates and activists claim should be protected. In your opinion, whose rights should be considered first? Whose rights should be considered last? Explain your answer.

Chapter 3

1. Kirsten Wonder Albrecht asserts that cultural competence tests deter available white families from adopting ethnic minority children. Leslie Doty Hollingsworth claims that recruitment efforts do not favor same-race adoptions among ethnic minorities. In your opinion, does Hollingsworth effectively counter Albrecht's argument? Explain.

2. Although their views of gay and lesbian adoptions conflict, Jill M. Crawford and Lynn D. Wardle suggest that two-parent households are advantageous to single-parent households. How do Crawford's and Wardle's reasons for supporting dual-parenting differ? Do their reasons share any similarities?

Chapter 4

1. Ira Carnahan argues that a compromise in adoption record laws can serve the adoptee's desire for background information and

the birth parent's request for confidentiality. Do you agree with the author? Why or why not?

2. In your opinion, who gains the most from open adoption? Who gains the most from closed adoption? Provide examples from the viewpoints to explain your answers.

3. The National Coalition for Child Protection Reform contends that family preservation efforts can help to expedite adoptions. On the other hand, Amanda Spake argues that such efforts hinder the adoption process. In your opinion, who makes the stronger argument? Why?

4. Consider the pros and cons of using the Internet to facilitate adoptions. Using these views, formulate an argument in which you support or oppose using the Internet to connect children with potential adoptive families.

Organizations to Contact

The editors have compiled the following list of organizations concerned with the issues debated in this book. The descriptions are derived from materials provided by the organizations. All have publications or information available for interested readers. The list was compiled on the date of publication of the present volume; the information provided here may change. Be aware that many organizations take several weeks or longer to respond to inquiries, so allow as much time as possible.

Abolish Adoption
PO Box 401, Palm Desert, CA 92261
website: www.abolishadoption.com
e-mail: info@abolishadoption.com

Abolish Adoption is an organization that petitions to end the practice of adoption. It believes that adoption is not in the child's best interests and violates human rights. Abolish Adoption also campaigns for open adoption records laws. Its publications include *The Ultimate Searchbook: Worldwide Adoption, Genealogy, and Other Search Secrets* by Lori Carangelo.

Adoption.com
800-ADOPT-HERE
website: http://adoption.com • e-mail: comments@adoption.com

Adoption.com is a web-based network of adoption organizations. It features profiles of prospective adoptive parents and adoptable children, and it addresses adoption issues such as unplanned pregnancy, international adoption, and adoption reunions. Several publications and magazines, such as the *2001 Adoption Guide* and *Adoption Today* magazine, are available at this site.

Bastard Nation (BN)
21904 Marine View Drive S, PMB 138, Des Moines, WA 98198
(415) 704-3166
website: www.bastards.org • e-mail: members@bastards.org

Bastard Nation is an adoptees' rights organization that campaigns to legalize adopted adults' access to records that pertain to their historical, genetic, and legal identity. It publishes the newsletter *Bastard Quarterly*.

Child Welfare League of America (CWLA)

440 First Street NW, Suite 310, 3rd Floor, Washington, DC 20001
(202) 638-2952 • fax: (202) 638-4004
website: www.cwla.org • e-mail: webweaver@cwla.org

CWLA, a social welfare organization concerned with setting standards for welfare and human services agencies, encourages research on all aspects of adoption. It publishes *Child Welfare: A Journal of Policy, Practice, and Program.*

Concerned United Birthparents (CUB)

PO Box 230457, Encinitas, CA 92023
(800) 822-2777 • fax: (760) 929-1879
website: www.cubirthparents.org
e-mail: info@CUBirthparents.org

CUB provides assistance to birth parents, works to open adoption records, and seeks to develop alternatives to the current adoption system. It helps women considering the placement of a child for adoption make an informed choice and seeks to prevent unnecessary separation of families by adoption. CUB publishes the monthly *Concerned United Birthparents-Communication.*

Families Adopting Children Everywhere (FACE)

PO Box 28058, Northwood Station, Baltimore, MD 21239
(410) 488-2656
website: www.face2000.org • e-mail: adopt2000@aol.com

FACE provides support to adoptive parents and families and promotes legislation advocating children's rights. It publishes the bimonthly *FACE Facts* magazine.

International Concerns for Children (ICCC)

911 Cypress Drive, Boulder, CO 80303
(303) 494-8333
website: www.iccadopt.org • e-mail: icc@boulder.net

ICCC helps those interested in adopting children from foreign countries. It acquaints prospective adoptive parents with ways to assist homeless children through sponsorship, fostering, and adoption. It publishes the quarterly *International Concerns Committee for Children Newsletter.*

National Adoption Information Clearinghouse (NAIC)

330 C Street SW, Washington, DC 20447
(703) 352-3488 • fax: (703) 385-3206
website: www.calib.com/naic/index.htm • e-mail: naic@calib.com

NAIC distributes publications on all aspects of adoption, including infant and international adoption, the adoption of children with special needs, and pertinent state and federal laws. For research, it provides a computerized information database containing titles and abstracts of books, articles, and program reports on adoption.

National Coalition for Child Protection Reform (NCCPR)

53 Skyhill Road, Suite 202, Alexandria, VA 22314
(703) 212-2006 (phone and fax)
website: www.nccpr.org • e-mail: info@NCCPR.org

The NCCPR is a group of professionals who have encountered the child welfare system in their professional capacities. It works to improve this system by changing policies concerning child abuse, foster care, and family preservation. Its publications include issue papers on orphanages, foster care, and family preservation efforts.

National Council for Adoption (NCFA)

1930 17th Street NW, Washington, DC 20009-6207
(202) 328-1200
website: www.ncfa-usa.org • e-mail: ncfadc@attglobal.net

Representing volunteer agencies, adoptive parents, adoptees, and birth parents, NCFA works to protect the institution of adoption and to ensure the confidentiality of all involved in the adoption process. It strives for adoption regulations that will ensure the protection of birth parents, children, and adoptive parents. Its biweekly newsletter, *Memo*, provides updates on state and federal legislative and regulatory changes affecting adoption. NCFA also publishes *Adoption Factbook III*.

Resolve, Inc.

1310 Broadway, Somerville, MA 02144-0744
(617) 623-1156 • fax: (617) 623-0252
website: www.resolve.org • e-mail: resolveinc@aol.com

Resolve, Inc. is a nationwide information network serving the needs of men and women dealing with infertility and adoption issues. It publishes fact sheets and a quarterly national newsletter containing articles, medical information, and book reviews.

Bibliography of Books

Salman Akhtar and Selma Kramer, eds.	*Thicker Than Blood: Bonds of Fantasy and Reality in Adoption.* Northvale, NJ: Jason Aronson, 2000.
Julie Berebitsky	*Like Our Very Own: Adoption and the Changing Culture of Motherhood, 1851–1950.* Lawrence: University of Kansas Press, 2000.
Barbara Birmingham-Brown	*Why Didn't She Keep Me?: Answers to the Questions Every Adopted Child Asks.* South Bend, IN: Diamond Communications, 1998.
Carolyn Campbell	*Together Again: True Stories of Birth Parents and Adopted Children United.* New York: Berkley Publishing Group, 1999.
E. Wayne Carp	*Family Matters: Secrecy and Disclosure in the History of Adoption.* Cambridge, MA: Harvard University Press, 2000.
Peter F. Dodds	*Outer Search/Inner Journey: An Orphan and Adoptee's Quest.* Pullayup, WA: Aphrodite Publishing Company, 1997.
Sherrie Eldridge	*Twenty Things Adopted Kids Wish Their Adoptive Parents Knew.* New York: Dell Books, 1999.
Madelyn Freundlich	*Adoption and Ethics, Volume 1.* Washington, DC: Child Welfare League of America, 2000.
Lois Gilman	*The Adoption Resource Book, Fourth Edition.* New York: HarperCollins, 1998.
James L. Gritter	*Lifegivers: Framing the Birthparent Experience in Open Adoption.* Washington, DC: Child Welfare League of America, 2000.
Timothy A. Hasci	*Second Home: Orphan Asylums and Poor Families in America.* Cambridge, MA: Harvard University Press, 1998.
Stephen Hicks and Jane McDermott, eds.	*Lesbian and Gay Fostering and Adoption: Extraordinary Yet Ordinary.* Philadelphia: Jessica Kingsley Publishers, 1998.
Patricia Irwin Johnson	*Adoption After Infertility.* Indianapolis, IN: Perspective Press, 1996.
Gregory C. Keck and Regina M. Kupecky	*Adopting the Hurt Child: Hope for Families with Special-Needs-Kids: A Guide for Parents and Professionals.* Colorado Springs, CO: Pinion Press, 1998.
Robert Klose	*Adopting Alyosha: A Single Man Finds a Son in Russia.* Jackson: University of Mississippi Press, 1999.

Mike Milotte	*Banished Babies*. Dublin, Ireland: New Island Books, 1997.
Stephen O'Connor	*The Orphan Trains: The Story of Charles Loring Brace and the Children He Saved and Failed*. Boston: Houghton Mifflin, 2001.
Sandra Patton	*BirthMarks: Transracial Adoption in Contemporary America*. New York: New York University Press, 2000.
Joyce Maguire Pavao	*The Family of Adoption*. Boston: Beacon Press, 1998.
Adam Pertman	*Adoption Nation: How the Adoption Revolution Is Transforming America*. New York: BasicBooks, 2000.
William L. Pierce, ed.	*The Adoption Factbook III*. Washington, DC: National Council for Adoption, 1999.
Bruce M. Rappaport	*The Open Adoption Book: A Guide for Adoption Without Tears*. New York: Hungry Minds, 1998.
Sharon E. Rush	*Loving Across the Color Line: A White Adoptive Mother Learns About Race*. Lanham, MD: Rowman and Littlefield, 2000.
Jayne E. Schooler and Betsy E. Keefer	*Telling the Truth to Your Adopted or Foster Child*. Westport, CT: Bergin and Garvey, 2000.
Kathleen Silber and Phylis Speedlin	*Dear Birthmother*. San Antonio, TX: Corona Publishing, 1998.
Rita J. Simon and Howard Altstein	*Adoption Across Borders: Serving the Children in Transracial and Intercountry Adoptions*. Lanham, MD: Rowman and Littlefield, 2000.
Rita J. Simon and Rhonda M. Roorda	*In Their Own Voices: Transracial Adoptees Tell Their Stories*. New York: Columbia Press, 2000.
LaVonne H. Stiffler	*Synchronicity and Reunion: The Genetic Connection of Adoptees and Birthparents*. Hobe Sound, FL: FEA Publishing, 1992.
Richard Tessler, Gail Gamache, and Liming Liu	*When West Meets East*. Westport, CT: Bergin and Garvey, 1999.
Amal Treacher and Ilan Katz	*The Dynamics of Adoption*. Philadelphia: Jessica Kingsley Publishers, 2000.
Jan L. Waldron	*Giving Away Simone*. New York: Anchor Books, 1997.

Index

abortion
  adoption chosen over, 34–35
  eliminating support for, 35–36
  and open adoption records, 150–51
  promoting adoption as alternative to, 39–40
  as cruel and punitive, 41
adoptees
  African American, 177–79
  on transracial adoptions, 89–90
  compared with nonadopted peers, 19
  disclosing information on, prior to adoption, 64–70
  educating, on their rights, 75
  focusing on future of, 24
  of gay and lesbian parents, 117–19
  grief of, 27, 28
  lifelong effects of separation from birth mother on, 47
  nondiscrimination of, 73
  and open adoption records, 151–52, 158
  in open adoptions
    are at greater risk, 135–36
    understanding of adoption by, 134–35
  protecting rights of, 73–74
  providing personal history to, 74–75
  providing services for, 77–78
  respecting, 75–76
  search for birth relatives, 77
  support and counseling for, 74
  see also transracial adoption
adoption
  advertising for, 51–52
  age of placement affecting success of, 21
  alternatives to
    assisting birth mothers with temporary problems, 30–31
    placing children with extended family or social circle, 28, 75–76
  barriers to, 33–35
  Chinese, number of, 152–53
  chosen over abortion, 34–35
  as a disgrace, 46–47
  as ethically and morally wrong, 26–27
  and family preservation, 169–71
  foster care to, 18, 173–74, 178–79, 182
  is not necessary, 27
  lives affected by, 31
  media portrayal on, 33
  and postplacement services, 75

  private vs. public, 173–74
  process of
    birth father excluded from, 56
    birth father's legal rights in, 60–61
    consent by birth parents in, 61
    counseling of birth mother in, as limited, 47–48
    deregulating, 37
    gay and lesbian couples walking away from, 104–105
    need for birth father involvement in, 61–62
    nondiscrimination of child in, 73
    privatizing, 37
    proposed reforms for, 48–53
    for transracial adoption, as difficult, 88–89
    see also adoption agencies; Internet adoption
  secrecy in, 142–43
  vs. serving best interests of children, 28–30
  and shame, 143
  support for, 18, 39
  see also individual types of adoption
Adoption 2002 initiative, 18
adoption agencies
  bases for liability of, 69
  choosing, 190
  disclosing information to adoptive families, 77
    benefits of, 64–65
    educating adoptive parents on, 69–70
    lack of, 65–67
    recommendation for, 67–69
    staff training for, 70–71
  educating adoptive parents on services available, 77–78
  responsiveness to families of color, 97–98
  and transracial adoptions, 92
  turning away gays and lesbians, 103
  see also adoption, process of
Adoption and Foster Care Analysis and Reporting System (AFCARS), 182
Adoption and Safe Families Act (1997), 104, 174, 176
Adoption Assistance and Child Welfare Act (1980), 103, 175
adoption records
  confidentiality of
    and abortion rates, 150
    adoptees on, 151–52
    need for, 156–58

and "safe-haven" laws, 152
disclosing previously confidential,
147–48
government should not regulate,
158–59
and interests of adoptees, 158
open
  and adoptees' rights, 52–53, 159–60
  debate on, 155
  influence of, on number of
    adoptions, 152–53
  organization promoting, 148–49
  and release of medical information,
    149–50
  and right to privacy, 155–56
Adoption Resource Center of
  Connecticut, 191
adoptive parents
  changing mind on adoption, 170
  choosing international over domestic
    adoption, 177–78
  in closed adoptions, 52
  of color, 97–98, 178
  on criticism of transracial adoptions,
    93
  cultural competence test for, 86–88
  disclosing information to, 64–70, 77
  educating prospective, 69–70, 77–78
  eligibility for, greater flexibility in, 94
  favoring open records, 157
  foster parents as, 22, 96–97
  as having power in adoptive
    relationships, 53–54
  Internet is useful tool for recruiting,
    182–84
  keeping out of the delivery room, 50
  number of prospective, 40–41
  in open adoptions
    breaking obligations, 53
    returning baby to birth parents,
      139–41
    unresolved grief of, 133
  potential pool of, 23
  sexual preference should not be
    criteria for, 105–106
  as victims of Internet fraud, 190–91,
    192
  see also gay and lesbian parents; single
    parents; transracial adoption
African Americans. See transracial
  adoption
Alabama, 147–48
Albrecht, Kirsten Wonder, 83
Allen, Richard, 128
Allen, Vickie, 128
American Public Human Services
  Association (APHSA), 185–86
Anderson, Carole, 44, 132

attachment disorder, 179

Babb, L. Anne, 72
Baby Jessica, 33
Baby Richard, 33
Baran, Annette, 130, 133
Barth, Richard, 24
Bartholet, Elizabeth, 17, 87, 178
Bastard Nation, 147–48, 150, 152, 153
Berry, Marianne, 135–36, 143
Biles, Rebecca, 106
biological parents
  anxieties of, in closed adoptions, 138
  changing mind in open adoptions,
    139–41
  consent by, 44–45, 51, 61
  disclosing background information
    on, 65, 66, 69
  and family preservation, 175–76
  foster care children developing ties
    with, 21
  see also birth fathers; birth mothers
biracial children. See transracial
  adoption
birth fathers
  caring concern by, 56–57
  counseling and support for, 57–58
  excluded from adoption process, 56
  legal rights of, 60–61
  need for involvement by, 58–59,
    61–62
  reasons for noninvolvement by,
    59–60
  see also biological parents
birth mothers
  adoption benefits, 36
  assisting with problems, vs. adoption,
    30–31
  biological connection with child, 49
  and birth fathers, 58–59, 61
  changing mind about adoption,
    50–51
  choices by, as a fundamental right, 40
  counseling for, 47–48, 49
  do not ask to be created, 53
  drug use by, 20
  grief of, 27–28
  hospital experiences of, 49–50
  and open adoption records, 150,
    157–58
  separation from child, lifelong effects
    of, 29, 47
  status of, in open adoptions, 46
  in open adoptions, 130, 131–33
  promoting adoption to, as cruel and
    punitive, 41
  see also biological parents
Blankman, Laura, 176

Blumenthal, Richard, 191
Borgenson, Dean, 58–59
Branham, E., 81–82
Brodzinsky, David, 135
Bush, Rosaline, 36

Carnahan, Ira, 146
Carp, E. Wayne, 152–53
Carter, Susan, 171
Castellucci, Denise K., 154
child abuse
    adopted children suffering from, 19
    and myth of classlessness, 163–65
    and poverty, 99–100
children
    cases of "neglect" of, 165–66
    of color, 98–100
    in foster care
        adoption benefits, 18–19, 20–22
        adoption harms, 19, 20
        biological connection with birth
            mother, 49
        of color, 98
        prospective adoptive parents for, 22
    severing connection with birth
        mother, consequences of, 29, 47
    with special needs, 173
        adoptive families bond with, 21
        and disclosure of background
            information, 64–65, 71
        and family preservation program,
            170
        finding adoptive parents for, 81,
            184, 186
        prospective adoptive parents for, 23
        subsidy for foster care, 177
    see also adoptees
Children's Bureau, 181
Child Welfare League of America
    (CWLA), 105–106
Clinton, Bill, 18, 174, 176
Clinton, Hillary, 41
Coats, Dan, 35
counseling
    for adopted child, 74
    for birth father, 57–58
    for birth mother, 47–48
crack babies, 20
Crawford, Jill M., 102
cultural competence test, 84, 86–88

Delaware, 148
Denmark, 123
Department of Children and Families
    (DCF), 190
Digre, Peter, 176–77
Dorner, Patricia Martinez, 134
drugs, 20

Faces of Adoption, 184–86
Fagan, Patricia F., 133
Families First program, 166–67
family, preservation of
    and adoption, 169–71
    campaign against, 162–63
    and cases of "neglect," 165–66
    as effective, 166–68
    and foster care, 163, 167, 175
    and kinship care, 176–77
    policy and legislation limiting, 179–80
    and "reasonable efforts," 175–76
Federal Opportunities Discretionary
    Grants Program, 184
Feldman, Charles, 184
foster care
    adoption cannot solve problems of,
        169
    adults who grew up in, 174–75
    age as factor in placement of, 179
    children in, waiting to be adopted,
        173
    and family preservation, 163, 167,
        175
    federal payment for, 175
    kinship care, 98, 176–77
    need to eliminate, 36
    number of children in, 163, 182
    placed into adoption from, 18
        number of, 173–74, 182
        white vs. African Americans from,
            178–79
    redesigned with best interests of
        children, 28–29
    and transracial adoption, 85–86, 88,
        96–97
Freundlich, Madelyn, 63

Gaither, Hal, 180
gay and lesbian parents
    adoption agencies turning away, 103
    adoption by
        and children's rights, 123–24
        creating less threatening arena for,
            111–12
        and homophobia, 110
        law review literature on, 114–15
        legalizing, 124–25
        opposition to, 106
        policy changes for, 109–10
        and serving best interests of child,
            106–108
    discriminatory attitudes toward,
        108–109
    effect of, on child's sexual
        development, 117–18
    and extramarital sexual relationships,
        119–20

vs. heterosexual parenting, 120–23
noticeable concerns in children of, 118–19
studies on, flaws in, 115–17
successful adoptions with, 106, 110–11
walking away from adoption, 104–105
Gelles, Richard, 174
Gilman, Thomas, 190
Glendon, Mary Ann, 124
Grape, Helen, 179
Greiner, Marley, 148–49
Gritter, James L., 49, 137
Guggenheim, Martin, 169, 170
Gutman, Jeremiah, 150

health care workers, 49–50
Heiser, Wendy, 58
Hill, Helen, 147
Hochman, Gloria, 177
Hollingsworth, Leslie Doty, 91, 164
Homebuilders family preservation program, 166, 170
homosexual parents. See gay and lesbian parents

Iceland, 123
Intensive Family Preservation Services (IFPS), 167, 168
intercountry adoptions. See international adoption
InterEthnic Adoption Amendment, 87, 88–89, 90
international adoption
adoptive parents' reasons for, 177–78
as avoiding open adoption, 52
children's rights in, 73
number of Chinese, 40–41
obtaining background information for, 66–67
vs. public adoptions, 174
rise in, 22–23, 92
Internet adoption
fraud in, 192
need for federal regulation of, 192–93
photolisting services for, 184–85
criteria for children listed on, 187
need for federal, 185–86
privacy and confidentiality of, 187–88
red flags to look for when using, 191
scandals on, 128
unethical facilitators on, 190–91, 192
as a useful tool for finding adoptive families, 182–84

Javaid, Ghazala, 117–18

Jensen, Sarah, 59–60
Johnson, Tina, 128, 192

Kaplan-Roszia, Sharon, 144
Kilshaw, Alan, 128, 191
Kilshaw, Judith, 128, 191
Kirk, Ray, 168

Lang, Susan S., 157
legislation
adoption-friendly, 35, 180
encouraging adoption, 18
on issuing birth certificate to adoptees, 156–57
lacking definition of "family," 103–104
on public adoption, 174
on releasing open adoption records, 147
"safe-haven," 152
on same-sex partnerships, 123–24
on transracial adoption, 84, 87–90, 94–95
Lewis, Karen Gail, 118–19
Lieberman, Alicia, 179
Lifton, Betty Jean, 26
Lindsay, Jeanne Warren, 55
Lowe, Heather, 45
Ludbrook, Robert, 27

maternity homes, 35
media, 33
medical information, 149–50
minorities
as adoptive parents, 97–98, 178
children in foster care, 98–100
see also transracial adoption
Mooney, Mary Libb, 192–93
Morgan, Ron, 149
Multiethnic Placement Act (1994), 94–95, 180

National Adoption Exchange, 184–85, 186
National Adoption Month, 34
National Adoption Week, 34
National Association of Black Social Workers (NABSW), 84, 85, 92, 178
National Coalition for Child Protection Reform, 161
National Council for Adoption, 40
National Incidence of Child Abuse and Neglect, 99
Nelson, Abbie, 138
New Zealand, 27
North American Council on Adoptable Children, 97
Norway, 123

Olasky, Marvin, 32
open adoption
    adopted child's understanding of,
        134–35
    adoption as wrenching undertaking
        before, 138
    adoptive family in, 133
    birth mother status in, 46
    birth mother's access to child in, 130
    as blending birth and adopting
        families, 133
    children are at greater risk in, 135–36
    and honor, 144–45
    legally enforcing agreements in, 53
    and open adoption records, 152–53
    providing background information
        in, 76
    transition from closed adoptions to,
        139–40
    as an unenforceable agreement,
        130–31
    unresolved grief in, 130, 131–33
open records. See adoption records
Oregon, 147, 158

Pannor, Reuben, 130, 133
Pelton, Leroy, 163
Perman, Adam, 60
Peterson, Lisa, 63
Pierce, William L., 129, 148, 149, 153,
    175
Pixley, Cornilous, 176
Pixley, Latrena, 176
Planned Parenthood, 35
Pollitt, Katha, 38
poverty
    and child abuse, 164–65
    and children of color, 98–100
    and family structure, 122–23
    helping birth mothers in, vs.
        adoption, 30
    and single-parenting, 122
Project Hustle, 179–80
public adoption. See family,
    preservation of; foster care

Rearick, Penny, 190
Robinson, Evelyn Burns, 25
Roles, Patricia, 131

same-sex partnerships. See gay and
    lesbian parents

Schwalm, Steve, 106
Seader, Mary Beth, 129
Shawyer, Joss, 26
siblings, 73
Silber, Kathleen, 134
Simon, Rita, 178
single parents
    adoption by, 81–82
    and poverty, 122
    preferred over adoption, 35
    as shameful, 36
Small Business Job Protection Act
    (1996), 95
Smith, Chris, 35
Spake, Amanda, 172
Spry, Michael, 141
Style, Mary Beth, 44
Sullivan, Ann, 175
Sweden, 123

Taubert, Alberta, 134
tax credit, 34, 39, 95
Taylor, Frances Grandy, 189
teen pregnancy, 40
Tennessee, 148
transracial adoption
    adoptees on, 89–90, 178
    advantages of, 87
    cultural competence test for, 86–88
    as difficult process, 88–89
    and foster care, 98
    increase in, 94
    legislation on, 84, 87, 90, 94–95
    lessening need for, 95–96, 100–101
    number of Chinese, 92
    obstacles to, 84–86
    opposition to, 92–93
        criticism of, 93–94, 95
    organization for, 84
    and poverty, 98–100
    social workers uncomfortable with,
        178

Van Zandt, Dede, 173
Van Zandt, Keith, 173
Verrier, Nancy, 29

Waldorf, Rachel, 58
Wardle, Lynn D., 113
Warnock, Mary, 125
Wecker, Tranda, 191
welfare, 35